S0-ARM-891

The Copernican Plan Evaluated:

The Evolution of a Revolution

Joseph M. Carroll, Ed.D.

With the full text of the evaluation of:

The Masconomet Regional High School Renaissance Program:
The First Implementation of the Copernican Plan

Dean K. Whitla, Ph.D.
Janine Bempechet, Ed.D.
Vito Perrone, Ph.D.
Barbara B. Carroll, Ed.D.

and the evaluations of Seven Copernican High Schools

Published by Copernican Associates, Ltd.
17 Andrews Road, Topsfield, MA. 01983
508-887-2688

Copyright ©1994 by Joseph M. Carroll

All rights reserved. No part of this publication may be reproduced or transmitted in any form or by any means, electronic or mechanical, including photocopy, or any information storage and retrieval system, without permission from the publisher.

Graphic Design and Composition by Octal Publishing, Inc.

Library of Congress Cataloging-in-Publication Data
CIP 94-94380

ISBN 0-9641442-0-4

Foreword

In this era of school reform, there are surprisingly few models that are worthy of consideration. The Copernican Plan and its first pilot program, The Renaissance program, are certainly high on this short list. There are several reasons why this program is most impressive.

The first reason is the basic Copernican concept. When a proposal comes along which increases students' "time on task", reduces class size, sharply reduces the daily numbers of students with whom each teacher must interact, simultaneously reduces the number of classes with which a student deals each day, and establishes a class structure that supports what research seems to be telling us about better instruction, one is most impressed. Since this proposal can be implemented without increasing per pupil expenditures, often a stumbling block to reform, one must take this proposal seriously.

The second reason is that the proposal included a strong evaluation component. When the Masconomet Evaluation Committee invited our team to evaluate the Renaissance program, we willingly accepted the assignment. Our enthusiasm arose, not simply because of the interest in the Copernican Plan and the qualities of the Renaissance program (which we believed had the promise to make a difference in students' lives), but also because someone was willing to have the program evaluated. This decision to evaluate rigorously is rare indeed. For how many school programs over the centuries, for how many hundreds of thousands of hours of instruction, for how many millions of student hours, for all of the rhetoric on school reform, for all of the proposed programs, how many have been evaluated? How many of our leading educational thinkers base their strong and often influential opinions on data? In a country where research is highly respected, why are these procedures so seldom used to evaluate public school outcomes?

There are several reasons. Many educators feel that short answer or multiple choice tests, often suggested as methods of measurement, seek only superficial thinking from students. While there is more than a modicum of truth in this, it is interesting that these test results are accepted as useful criteria in college admissions—colleges where we expect serious scholarly work. A second limitation of program evaluations expressed by many educators is that achievement, no matter how it is measured, depends not upon what happens in the classroom but on the home environments from which students come. We therefore should not judge harshly a teacher or a school whose students do poorly because these students may well come from intellectually impoverished homes. It is true that typical assessments of student outcomes are generally correlated with parental background, but since, in the evaluation process, we can introduce controls for the formative experiences of children, the value added by the school can be isolated and identified. Since there are many developmental evaluation procedures to be used which can meet these needs, there is little reason for any educator not to find an acceptable methodology for his or her program's evaluation objectives.

Frankly, American education lags behind much of the world not because we lack ideas but because we do not know which ones are the most effective. It has been a pleasure to work with the group involved with the Renaissance program and with Joe Carroll and his Copernican Plan because they had the courage not only to try a different program but to put it through the evaluation crucible. The Copernican Plan Evaluated sends a message to those concerned about our schools that the school reform movement must become research based and centered on evaluation. These Copernican results show that useful research and research methodology are available, and when they are properly used in planning, implementing and evaluating programs, very good things can happen to students and schools. My hat is off to those associated with these Copernican programs and to the book that Dr. Carroll has written chronicling these events.

Dean K. Whitla
Cambridge, Massachusetts

Contents

Acknowledgements

The inherent risk in recording those to whom one is indebted for assistance in completing a book is that of overlooking someone's contribution. So let me begin with an apology to the unrecognized colleague, and then proceed to acknowledge the rest.

This book includes in appropriate sections the names of people who were associated with different programs. I hope they will consider their inclusion as an acknowledgement of their importance in developing this document. However, a special recognition must be accorded Dean Whitla, who headed the team from Harvard that evaluated the first Copernican pilot program, the Renaissance Program at the Masconomet Regional School District. This evaluation is presented in detail in this book. However, Dean's assistance did not end with the evaluation of the Renaissance Program. He was a constant source of support and encouragement in the long process of developing this book. He reviewed the evaluation data of each school and did all of the statistical work which is so important to this study. He often gave me time which I'm sure added to his long days as Director of Harvard University's Office of Instructional Research and Evaluation. Dean understands the importance of solid evaluation and also its limitations, and this work benefited from his discerning mind. I was so pleased that he would write the foreword for this book.

Janine Bempechet, an assistant professor at the Harvard Graduate School of Education, and one of the major contributors to the evaluation of the Renaissance Program, was also helpful in reading the draft of the section on the Renaissance Program. She has been very supportive of this effort to evaluate the impact of the Copernican Plan; her help is much appreciated.

Dave Donaval, a gifted teacher and the person selected by his colleagues as the leader of the Renaissance Team, also read a draft of this book and made suggestions which were quite helpful.

Bob Sperber, a professor of education at Boston University and a member of the management team that university established to manage the Chelsea Public Schools, was the person who invited me to meet with the administrators of Chelsea High School, which resulted in Chelsea's TRIMESTER Program. He has been most supportive, and his help is much appreciated. Working with Bob was Peter Greer, who left his position of Dean of the Boston University School of Education to be superintendent of the Chelsea schools. He was superintendent during the time covered by this evaluation and was supportive of the difficult decision to introduce the TRIMESTER Program.

Harold "Doc" Howe, former U.S. Commissioner of Education and a senior lecturer at the Harvard Graduate School of Education, has been a supporter of the Copernican Plan since he came upon a copy of my Copernican Plan Concept Paper in 1984. He undertook the arduous task of reading a much too long, early draft of this book, and he made several important suggestions, including the inclusion of a statement from the principals or other appropriate administrators of each of the schools which were being evaluated. His wisdom and consistent support is deeply appreciated.

Thanks to all.
JMC

Preface

In the fall of 1983, I distributed a document to the staff and school community of the Masconomet Regional School District called *The Copernican Plan: A Concept Paper Concerning the Restructuring of Secondary Education* at the Masconomet Regional School District. This document was the result of almost two decades of interest in the relationship between time and learning, beginning in the 1960's when I was Assistant Superintendent of the District of Columbia Public Schools. Since then, the ideas which I presented in that concept paper had evolved slowly, somewhat unevenly and eclectically. I had finally put it all together. My enthusiasm was not shared by all the Masconomet community, which was no surprise. "Restructuring" wasn't a hot topic at that time; Masconomet had an excellent reputation as a strong academic school and there weren't too many people who felt the need for major change. Still, in 1989, we were able to initiate a pilot program at Masconomet to test the basic Copernican concepts.

About the same time, The Regional Laboratory for Educational Improvement of the Northeast & Islands published a much expanded version of that concept paper as a book entitled *The Copernican Plan: Restructuring The American High School*. The concepts and the book were well received by the nation's educational community. Harold Howe wrote in the foreword of the book that "If the National Commission on Excellence in Education, which prepared the well-known document *A Nation at Risk*, had published Joseph Carroll's *The Copernican Plan* as a companion piece, the school reform movement in the United States would be far ahead of where it is now." The January 1990 KAPPAN featured a long article on the book. In July, 1990, a special edition of the U.S. News and World Report, dedicated to "The best in America", selected the Boston University contract to manage the troubled Chelsea Public Schools as the best program, but noted that The Copernican Plan was often mentioned by the 200 persons who participated in this decision, and this was the only other program mentioned. Articles appeared in many educational publications and also in newspapers including the New York Times and The Christian Science Monitor. The recognition was welcome. And a number of schools were planning to implement Copernican type programs. But this was a plan; a plan based on my reading of the research and some limited, non traditional experience. Would it work? Would it actually have a beneficial impact on the performance of students in typical high schools? That question needed to be viewed in the context of the history of "innovation" in our nation's schools.

Unevaluated or poorly evaluated proposals have often become accepted as the first step towards educational nirvana and have been adopted by many schools, sometimes with educationally disappointing results. The recurring waves of "innovations", each accompanied by an appropriate lexicon of new "buzz" words, too often expend immense resources in ineffective and sometimes less effective programs. To add to the professional damage, the programs that actually may be effective usually lack documentation necessary to demonstrate improvements and often give way to the weight of educational inertia, of adherence to the perception of safety in the status quo. This history of failed change has caused many educators to talk change but avoid action, and it has contributed greatly to the public's loss of faith in this nation's schools. I did not want the Copernican Plan to be another such program. I was confident that this plan would prove to be effective; however, if it did not make a difference, if it did not result in distinctly better education for students, then it should either be modified or terminated.

The only defense against educational faddism and its "anecdotal evaluation" is a sound evaluation centered on testing whether the program, in this case The Copernican Plan, can demonstrate it has met its claims for improved performance of students. This book is intended to provide solid, research-based answers to these questions.

It is my hope that this work may help to reorient this nation's restructuring efforts from its present process base and political orientation to become research based and evaluation oriented. This change addresses the essence of educational accountability; for nothing, absolutely nothing has happened in education until it happens to a student.

If this book helps you in your effort to improve the educational opportunities of the children in your charge, I will be most pleased. If you will share your plans and experiences or join in planning with neighboring schools, I will be delighted. For my purpose in writing is to foster a Copernican revolution in our nation's secondary schools.

JMC

Introduction

I have bad news and good news. The bad news is that our schools, and more particularly our high schools, are in serious trouble and may be replaced by new institutions of choice, both public and private, primarily because our efforts are not resulting in the development of either a workforce capable of competing with those of other industrialized nations or a citizenry capable of meeting its critically important responsibilities under our form of government. The good news is that all we have to do is apply what research tells us about better instruction and we can meet those demands. Furthermore, we can do it within our present systems, without "Japanizing" or "Germanizing" our schools, but by building upon cultural values which have served our nation well over many years.

What values are these? A willingness to challenge the status quo. Keeping our political values in focus at all times eg: freedom, equality, fairness, and constant concern for each individual. Intelligent application of what we know, eg: turning basic research into applied research and being willing to learn from others. And applying to the organization and management of our schools concepts of efficiency and accountability. We can do it our way. How? Read on.

This book is centered on evaluations and research based upon the concepts presented in *The Copernican Plan*, a plan for restructuring high schools which was developed in 1983.[1] An overview of *The Copernican Plan* may be useful in putting this book into proper perspective.

First, why call it *The Copernican Plan*? The name is appropriate. Nicolaus Copernicus was a 16th century scholar whose major contribution was his explanation of the movements of the planets. The movements of the planets had been studied for centuries. Copernicus's contrubution was simple, but fundamental. If these planetary movements are studied assuming the sun as the center of the universe, as universe was then defined, all of the measurements made sense. Studying them on the assumption that the earth was the center, nothing made sense. His findings resulted in what is known as the Copernican Revolution; indeed, the use of the word revolution to mean an uprising stems from the title of his book: The Revolution of the Heavenly Orbs.[2] Copernicus's theory encountered tremendous resistance. On the practical side, everyone could see the sun rise in the east and set in the west; on a much more serious level, that God had made the world and intended that man dominate it was an article of faith. Copernicus's simple change in perspective was therefore considered both incorrect and dangerous.

The Copernican Plan also challenges what has become an article of educational faith, the Carnegie unit, which has dominated the organization of secondary instruction for almost a century. Under the Carnegie structure, teachers typically teach five, approximately 45-minute classes and must deal with about 125 students each day. Indeed, the number of students taught very often increase to 150 or even 180 students per day. The 45-minute class often is utilized for every subject, which further complicates the problem of time in laboratory oriented subjects. Virtually all of the research on better instruction emphasizes greater individualization, greater personalization of instructuion.[3] But secondary school teachers are caught in a structure which supports lecture centered instruction, a large group form of instruction, and which sharply limits their efforts to individualize. The teacher cannot effectively implement what research tells us about better instruction under this structure.[4]

The Carnegie structure impacts students as well. Students typically enroll in six classes each day which are usually taught for a 180 days or a school year. In a typical high school with a seven-period day, a home room, and a lunch period, students will be in nine different locations with nine very different activities, all in an approximately six-and-a-half hour day; if the student has physical education, he or she may also have changed clothes twice and showered once. Whether the subject is English, art, or science, it is taught in approximately 45-minute classes. This is a procrustean structure which is impersonal, and certainly prevents the teacher from working closely with each student every day. Indeed, a student may go through an entire day, or several days, without having a meaningful interaction with a teacher.

In summation, there is nothing wrong with the traditional, Carnegie structure except that it is a structure under which teachers can't teach effectively and students can't learn effectively. Otherwise its fine! More seriously, its only justification is that it has become traditional; it is one of the few dominant characteristics of todays world that is familiar to the students, their parents, and their grandparents (and I could add great grandparents for those who have longevity)! But customs and traditions do not engender challenge or criticism; they are self justifying, and they do not yield easily to change.

The Copernican change is a fundamental change in the use of time eg: classes taught in much longer periods—90 minutes, 2 hours, or 4 hours per day—and which meet for only part of the school year—30 days, 45 days, 60 days or 90 days. Students are enrolled in significantly fewer classes each day and teachers deal with significantly fewer classes and students each day. The purpose of this schedule change is to create a classroom environment which fosters vastly improved relationships between teachers and students and also much more manageable workloads for both teachers and students. In theory, improved teacher/student relationships and more manageable workloads should result in more successful schools.

What can we expect to gain by making this Copernican change in the daily and annual schedule? The Copernican Plan summarized the advantages that should be gained as follows:

> "Virtually every high school in this nation can decrease its average class size by 20 percent; increase its course offerings or number of sections by 20 percent; reduce the total number of students with whom a teacher works each day by 60 to 80 percent; provide students with regularly scheduled seminars dealing with complex issues; establish a flexible, productive instructional environment that allows effective mastery learning as well as other practices recommended by research; get students to master 25 to 30 percent more information in addition to what they learn in the seminars; and do all of this within approximately present levels of funding."[5]

The *Copernican Plan* proposes a series of other changes; Interest/Issues Seminars; evaluation based on a Mastery Credit System; Individual Learning Plans (ILP's); Multiple diplomas and a new credit system with two types of credits; and a major emphasis on dejuvenilizing our high schools. But the achievement of these changes—or any other of the many interesting changes proposed for our high schools—is dependent upon fundamental changing of the classroom environment for teachers and students. This is the Copernican change upon which the success of virtually all other changes is dependent.

How do we test these Copernican concepts? The productive unit in education is the individual school, and that is the natural laboratory in which to assess the effectiveness of educational proposals, including this Copernican proposal. The first section of this book will deal, conceptually, with research and evaluation and will present the evaluation of the first attempt to implement the Copernican Plan at Masconomet Regional High School in Boxford, Massachusetts. The second section will build on the evaluation of the Masconomet program and will test the conclusions of this evaluation against the evaluated experience of seven other high schools that initiated versions of a Copernican structure. The third section will summarize the results and analyze the meaning of these results. These evaluations will concentrate totally on what happened to students, will be performance based, and will include some educationally spectacular results, including academic results.

The final section presents the considerable potential of this experience for the achievement of this nation's educational goals. It also considers the opportunity for a revolutionary improvement in the quality of service our high schools can provide our nation and the critical importance of seizing this opportunity.

So let us begin.

Part I

The Evaluation of the Renaissance Program

The First Copernican Pilot Program

"There is nothing more difficult to take in hand, more perilous to conduct, or more uncertain in its success, than to take the lead in the introduction of a new order of things"[6]

Nicolo Machiavelli

Machiavelli was right. The Copernican Plan was the result of about twenty years of interest and experimentation in three school districts concerning the problems of our high schools. This work was formalized into a very long concept paper in 1983, while I was superintendent at the Masconomet Regional School District in Massachusetts. It took six years to negotiate through to implementation of a pilot program in 1989. The pilot program, which was named the Renaissance Program, had endured a long, tense, and sometimes stormy gestation period and this pilot program survived for only two years.(Attachment A: pp.5-10, 45) But this eight years of experience from conception to termination is a very different story than the one which needs to be presented here, albeit it is one which has interested quite a number of people. The record of the Renaissance Program and to a very considerable extent, the future of the Copernican Plan rests in the evaluation of those two years of experience, in what happened to students as a result of this change; Again, absolutely nothing has happened in education until it has happened to a student.

Before we consider the evaluation of the Renaissance Program, however, it may be helpful to consider the role of research and evaluation in education.

THE RELATIONSHIP BETWEEN RESEARCH AND EVALUATION

Let us first consider the status and usefulness of educational research and research based evaluation. Research provides no formula that absolutely guarantees a particular level of instructional success to all students, any more than medical research absolutely guarantees successful treatment of a particular malady for every category of patient. But with constant review of findings, educators like physicians can improve their success rates, which will benefit more and more students. Educational evaluation should use the tools of the researchers to evaluate their programs. But there is a difference between evaluation and research.

Researchers, quite properly, view their results narrowly and are reluctant to project the application of their findings beyond the experimental parameters of the research. But the teacher or administrator, also quite properly, must make decisions based on the weight of evidence. Weight of evidence does not require a specific level of statistical significance. However, research findings which are supported by higher levels of statistical significance provide much stronger guidance and thus should be major factors in making decisions concerning various options. To be effective, educators must exercise informed judgment about the meaning of findings and how they can provide direction in developing more productive educational programs. And most important, be aware that to decide not to change is a decision that what is being done now is better than any alternative. Be sure that the justification of the present program meets the same standards as are applied to proposed changes. Remember, while it is possible to change without improving, it is impossible to improve without changing.

THE COPERNICAN PLAN: RESEARCH BASED
AND EVALUATION DRIVEN

The Copernican Plan is research based in its planning and evaluation driven in its implementation. Let us consider these concepts as they applied to this program.

Educational planning should be guided by instructional research; it should be research-based. Planners should try to establish conditions which will allow for the effective implementation of instructional strategies that have been shown to be most effective. "The Copernican Plan Concept Paper", presented in 1983, devoted 17 pages to "AN ANALYSIS OF THE IMPACT OF THE COPERNICAN PLAN ON THE ABILITY OF A SCHOOL TO CREATE CONDITIONS WHICH RESEARCH SHOWS TO BE ASSOCIATED WITH EFFECTIVE SCHOOL-ING".[7] In 1989, in "THE COPERNICAN PLAN, Restructuring The American High School", a chapter entitled "WHY THE COPERNICAN PLAN WORKS" expanded on the concept paper and established a research base for this proposed restructuring. It included an analysis of successful experience of nontraditional education programs, analyzed findings from behavioral psychology, cognitive psychology, and effective schools research, and compared their probability of implementation in both traditional and Copernican structures. The resulting Copernican Plan projected the probability of significantly improved learning on the basis of this research. In summation, the research supported the position that changing to a Copernican schedule would very significantly improve the relationship between teachers and students, would provide much more manageable workloads for both teachers and students, and would establish a classroom schedule that would foster implementation of better instruction. However, until regular high schools actually implemented a Copernican structure and the results of this change were evaluated, it was only a plan.

Once a research based plan is developed, its implementation should be evaluation driven. The following sections will present evaluations of the impact of implementation of the Copernican Plan in eight high schools, which represent many different communities and different Copernican schedules. All of the evaluations will concentrate on how students prospered and performed in these schools as a result of the implementation of a Copernican structure. Research methodologies are utilized in these evaluations; they will be presented later, in the context of these evaluations.

There is one fundamental, common question which is basic to every evaluation: do students function as well and learn as effectively under a Copernican structure as they now do under a traditional, Carnegie structured school? The baseline data, the information against which progress or lack of progress must be measured, must come from student performance data under traditional, Carnegie schedules; the experimental variable is the implementation of a Copernican schedule; the impact of that experimental variable must be measured by comparing the baseline performance data with the same performance data from students functioning and learning under a Copernican schedule; and research methodologies should be utilized in analyzing the data and in interpreting the results.

INITIATING THE EVALUATION

Let us now consider the evaluation of the Renaissance Program, the first Copernican pilot program, which was implemented at the Masconomet Regional High School in Boxford, Massachusetts. The following sections will describe how the evaluation was organized, how the evaluation team was selected, introduce you to the evaluation team, list the questions which that team was asked to answer, and will present their answers to those questions.

Objectivity was essential to effective evaluation of the Renaissance Program. Since the program had supporters and detractors, both groups had to be fairly represented in developing the evaluation so that the objectivity that was needed was not only achieved but was generally accepted. It was also important to have the evaluators on board before the program began. Thus, in advance of the implementation of the program, the Masconomet Regional School Committee established a special Renaissance Program Evaluation Committee comprised of a school committee member who supported the Renaissance Program (Renpro) and one who opposed it; a teacher selected by the Renpro teachers and one selected by the Teachers Association, which opposed the program; a parent who had a student in the program and one who elected to stay with the traditional program (Tradpro); and a member selected by the department heads, who were organized in a separate unit from the teachers. A number of administrators met with the committee and provided support for its work but were not members and could not vote. These were the superintendent, the administrator responsible for computer operations, and the director of guidance. The latter two staff were in a position to help evaluators gather and organize data which would be needed for their work.

The Renaissance Evaluation Committee developed a set of specifications stating the questions that they needed answered by the evaluators and actively sought proposals from leading university professionals as well as from educational consultants having appropriate experience. After reviewing a number of proposals, they conducted interviews with four finalists and then selected an outstanding team from Harvard University to conduct the evaluation.

This team was regularly referred to as the "Harvard Team" and the resulting evaluation report was called the "Harvard evaluation", and thus those terms will be used in this book. In the interest of clarity, it should be noted that the contract was with faculty members of Harvard, but not with Harvard.

THE EVALUATION TEAM

The names of those conducting this evaluation are in the Harvard Team's report, which is presented in its entirety as Attachment A, but their resumes are not. Since the quality of the report can be no better than the competence of those who developed it, some comment on their qualifications is appropriate.

> **Dr. Dean Whitla**, who had the lead role, has been the Director of Harvard University's Office of Instructional Research and Evaluation for over 25 years and carries two faculty appointments including one in the

Graduate School of Education, where he is the Director of the Counseling and Consulting Psychology Program. He is responsible for evaluating the University's academic programs including each freshman class, and he is the senior member of the Harvard Admissions Committee. He has conducted about 200 evaluations of elementary and secondary education programs as a consultant.

Dr. Vito Perrone heads the teacher education programs for the Harvard Graduate School of Education. He is also a Senior Fellow at the Carnegie Foundation for the Advancement of Teaching. Dr. Perrone is a gifted teacher, has a distinguished record as an educational researcher and is a perceptive analyst of the climate and practice of education.

Dr. Janine Bempechat is an assistant professor on the faculty of the Harvard Graduate School of Education. She is an excellent researcher, with particular credentials in the area of student motivation. Dr. Bempechat played major roles in planning and managing the evaluation.

Dr. Barbara B. Carroll (no relation to the author), a member of the staff of Harvard's Office of Instructional Research and Evaluation, did the very considerable statistical analyses for the Renaissance Program evaluation.

The field work, classroom observations, and interviewing were directed by Dr. Bempechet. She was assisted by Gabrielle Bamford, Miya Omari, and Paul Schlictman, all excellent, experienced professionals who were also Harvard Doctoral Students.

This was, indeed, an impressive evaluation team.

THE HARVARD EVALUATION

Attachment A presents, verbatim, the Harvard team's evaluation of the first Copernican pilot, the Renaissance Program. It should be noted that the Renpro followed the "B" Schedule of the Copernican Plan[8], with adaptions required for a pilot program organized as a school-within-a-school. Exhibit 1, which is found on the following page, presents the basic schedule developed for the program. The first year, the Renpro was for ninth grade students only; the second year had both ninth and tenth grade classes. The Harvard Evaluation describes the Renaissance Program in considerable detail (pp. 110-113).

The Harvard evaluators developed several bases for their findings (pp. 113-114). Questionnaires were given to both Renpro and Tradpro parents, students and teachers. Thus they were able to compare responses from those who chose the Renpro with those who chose to stay with the traditional program. These questionnaires were followed by interviews from a sample of each group, in order to gain insights into the reasons behind the responses to the questionnaires. The midterm and final exams for all courses were exactly the same for both groups of students, to provide a basis for academic evaluations. Other evaluative approaches will be discussed in the context of presenting answers to each of the questions addressed by the evaluation.

6   *The Copernican Plan Evaluated*

Exhibit 1
The Renaissance Program
Typical Students Program

Yearly Daily	Trimester I		Trimester II		Trimester III	
Block I	English		Social Studies		Art *or* Keyboard Computer Elective	
Block II	Mathematics		Foreign Language		Physical Science	
Period 5	Possible all year elective or Chorus/Band					
Period 6*	Sem I	FLEP	Sem II	FLEP	Sem III	Ind. Study	Sem IV	Ind. Study	Sem V	FLEP	Sem VI	FLEP
Period 7	Extra help on alternative days with Block I and Block II teachers					

*Each Sem, FLEP, and Ind. Study period was scheduled for three weeks. FLEP means Foreign Language Enrichment Program.

The following sections present the major questions which the Harvard team was to try to answer and the team's findings concerning each of these questions.

1. *Will the students be able to function effectively in long "macroclasses" of about two hours?*

   Many predicted that all but perhaps the most able students would get bored or "burned out" trying to concentrate on one subject for that long a period of time.

   The Findings: The evaluators reviewed the two years of student data and came to the following conclusions: "Renaissance students were better known by their teachers, were responded to with more care, did more writing, pursued issues in greater depth, enjoyed their classes more, felt more challenged, and gained deeper understandings. Students can move from classes of 46 minutes to those of 118 minutes and back again. They are more flexible when it comes to length of class than is normally assumed, although Renaissance students preferred the longer class periods. Concentration on only two classes in much longer periods, aided by reduced class size, markedly improves the interpersonal relationships that develop between teacher and student, and between student and student" (p. 132).

   This conclusion does not mean that there were no student concerns. There were students who decided to leave the program as the second year began.

The Harvard Evaluation   7

Their reasons for leaving, with one exception, did not involve the longer class period. The competition between the programs and the controversy concerning the program had a negative impact on students, both Renpro and Tradpro. Student responses are specifically addressed on pages 117 to 118, 123 to 125, 127, and 130 to 131.

2. *Will the teachers find the intensity of teaching in roughly two hour classes draining; will they suffer "burn out"?*

   The Findings: "Renaissance teachers were excited about their teaching. They felt rejuvenated and believed they were teaching students more productively than ever. We learned that teachers of any level of seniority who get involved in developing a new program can become rededicated to teaching and give more time and energy to their students than previously. Simple changes in the length of class periods and in class size can in themselves invite teachers to re-think their pedagogical styles" (p. 113). This summary statement reflects a very high level of unanimity among the Renaissance teachers. Teacher reactions are presented on pages 114 to 115, 118 to 120, 127 to 128, and 160 to 163. The last reference is a long statement written and signed by the Renpro teachers in support of their program.

   It should be noted that the Tradpro teachers felt stressed by the competition presented by the Renpro. The competitive pressures created by a partial school or school-within-a-school approach was a negative factor felt by both Renpro and Tradpro teachers.

3. *Will the students learn as much as they would under the traditional structure?*

   This was a major criticism concerning the Renpro, because the Renpro classes the first year had only 100 hours to "cover" the curriculum while the traditional program provided 139 hours over a traditional, 180 day school year; in the second year, it was 118 hours vs. 139; and 118 hours vs. 162 hours in the traditional program for an honors science course with a double lab period once in every six day cycle. Most teachers and many other critics were certain that the course material could not be covered in that much less time.

   The Findings: "To make valid comparisons between these two groups of students, their academic strengths as they began their respective ninth grade programs were compared. Students' scores on the eighth grade Iowa Test of Basic Skills indicated that the traditional students had significantly higher reading scores than did the Renaissance students. The Traditional students also scored higher in mathematics, but not significantly so" (p. 122).

   "The academic performance of each program was analyzed by comparing the midterm exams of each Renaissance trimester with the midyear exams of the Traditional students, and the final exams of each trimester with the traditional end-of-year exams. Teachers in both programs used the same curriculum, and the same midterm and final exams were administered to students" (p. 122).

"Renpro students had significantly fewer hours of class (100 v. 139 hours in the first year: 118 vs. 139 hours in the second year, and 118 vs. 162 hours for science with the traditional laboratory period). While there were differences in scores between students in the two programs, these differences essentially balanced out. The results were comparable, even though there were significant differences in 'time on task.' In addition, Renpro students had more opportunities for academic enrichment (more courses, seminars, independent studies and FLEP programs) than did the Tradpro, and actually completed 13% more course credits than did Tradpro students" (p. 132). These test results are summarized in the following table:

A SUMMARY OF RENPRO-TRADPRO ACADEMIC COMPARISON OF MIDTERM AND FINAL EXAMINATIONS 1989-90 AND 1990-91

RESULTS IN WHICH THE DIFFERENCES WERE NOT SIGNIFICANT	49
RESULTS IN WHICH THE DIFFERENCES WERE SIGNIFICANT FAVORING:	
RENPRO (COPERNICAN)	11
TRADPRO (TRADITIONAL)	14
TOTAL COMPARISONS	74

In summation, although the Renpro students were found to be less able than the Tradpro students, based on their previous verbal and mathematics records, they performed as well as the Tradpro students on their examinations and completed 13% more courses plus a seminar program than did the Tradpro students.

4. Will the students retain as much of what they learn?

Critics pointed out that students in the Renpro could take a course in the first trimester in one year and might not take the next sequential course until the third trimester of the following year, a gap of 15 months as compared to the traditional summer vacation gap of 3 months. They believed students would forget a great deal more in such a long period and that this would seriously hamper their academic progress.

The Findings: There were really two measures of retention in this evaluation. The first measure was inherent in the structure of this pilot program because it required Renpro students to begin one third of their courses after a gap of three months since their previous course in the subject (June to September), one third after six months (June to December), and one third after a gap of nine months (June to March). All the Tradpro students began their next sequential course after the traditional June to September gap. In the second year of the program, the second year students were scheduled without consideration to the trimester in which they had taken a course in a subject during the first year, and some students had gaps of up to 15 months since their previous course in a subject. Thus, the academic findings presented in question 3 above, that the Renpro students performed as well academically as the Tradpro students, is strong evidence that the longer gaps between sequential courses were not instructionally significant.

The academic results were very impressive and certainly did not reflect any problems, including any problems with the gap between sequential levels of courses. But it was an indirect rather than a direct evaluation of the impact of the differences in the gap between sequential courses in the two programs. The Harvard evaluators decided to test retention levels in the two programs directly. " During the second year, in September, December and March, comparisons were made of the retention of material studied during the first year. These comparisons, referred to as "gap tests," were administered from 3 months to 15 months after the courses ended" (p. 128). "Even when one takes into account that gap test results were compared without regard to the time lapse between final exam and gap test (which should favor the traditional program), there were no consistent significant differences that favored students in one program over students in the other" (p. 129). Exhibit 2, which is found on the following page, presents a summary of these gap test findings. The evaluators concluded: "The gap tests, administered to determine levels of retention of course material over time, also showed that the Renaissance and the Traditional program students had comparable levels of retention" (p. 132).

This finding is consistent with the reports from independent schools and non traditional programs that utilized Copernican type schedules,[9] and is consistent with the basic research concerning retention. This research will be presented in Part III of this book.

Please carefully observe that this finding, with the findings to question 3 concerning academic achievement, resulted in the evaluators concluding: "The Renaissance Program met its academic objectives" (p. 132).

5. *Will the quality of instruction under the Renpro be in as much depth as that of the traditional program?*

The critics believed that the pressure to "cover" the curriculum in significantly less time would result in superficial learning, without addressing more complex questions which develop higher order thinking and problem solving capability in students. And developing these abilities in students is a national as well as local objective.

The Findings: There was a serendipitous evaluation and also, a special, well structured evaluation designed to test the impact of the Renpro on higher order thinking and problem solving ability of students. The first, serendipitous evaluation came about when Renpro students scored significantly higher (statistically) than did the Tradpro students on the essay portion of an English examination. Since the Tradpro students had been found to be significantly

The Copernican Plan Evaluated

more able in verbal performance in the year before the Renpro began, this result was questioned; those questioning this result noted that the teachers were scoring their own exams (essays) and evaluating compositions can be less than objective. To address this criticism, the Harvard team took both the Renpro and Tradpro student essays to an experienced and excellent English teacher, who was a doctoral student, and had the essays regraded, taking care not to identify the essays with one or the other program. The finding: "Analysis of the rescored essays confirmed that the Renaissance students performed significantly higher than did the Traditional students" (p. 122). But is improved ability to write a measure of higher order thinking? Research shows "that writing may well be a unique way to learn since the process inherently demands acts of analysis and synthesis that mark higher order intellectual functioning".[10] Thus, this finding is a valid and statistically significant indication that the Renpro was developing these desired capabilities to a significantly greater degree than was the Tradpro.

The second assessment came from research concerned with higher order thinking skills and problem solving. This research was being conducted at the

Exhibit 2
A Comparison of Retention
1989/90 RENPRO and TRADPRO Results Based Upon "Gap Testing"

Time Gaps	Differences Favoring		Degree of Difference	
	RENPRO	TRADPRO	Significant	Not Significant
TRAD 3 Months with REN 3 Months	4	4	0	8
TRAD 6 Months with REN 6 Months	4	3	0	7
TRAD 3 Months with REN 6 Months	4	5	2 (favoring TRADPRO)	7
TRAD 3 Months with REN 9 Months	0	9	3 (favoring TRADPRO)	6
TRAD 6 Months with REN 9 Months	1	2	0	3
TRAD 6 Months with REN 12 Months	1 (1 tie)	2	0	3

Harvard Graduate School of Education, and the evaluation team was able to make it available for the evaluation of the Renaissance Program. Renpro and Tradpro students who had completed two years in their respective programs were organized into groups of two and three students and each group was given either a science related task or a social sciences related task. The students were video taped as they addressed their task. Each student was evaluated on three factors shown to be associated with higher order thinking and problem-solving. The evaluators were from the University and were not aware of the program in which each student participated. In 16 of 20 comparisons, the Renpro students were rated more highly than their Tradpro peers. "When the sign test was applied to these data collectively, the Renpro students performed significantly better than Tradpro students ($p<0.001$)" (pp. 164-167). For those not familiar with statistical concepts, this finding means that if there really was no difference in the impact of these two programs on the development of these skills, the chance of getting a sample of students who would score this differently is less than one in a thousand. The evaluators concluded: "Oral exams assessing students' capacities for thinking through problems and working cooperatively showed that former Renaissance students performed significantly better than Traditional students on these dimensions" (p. 132).

In a profession where one chance in twenty is considered statistically significant, these two independent evaluations reinforce each other and together, strongly support the premise that a Copernican type program will develop higher order thinking and improved problem solving skills in students more effectively than will traditionally structured programs.

THE BOTTOM LINE: On all five of these major questions, this Copernican pilot program was found to be significantly more effective than its Tradpro counterpart. Does this mean that there were no problems? "The Renaissance Program was not perfect. Teachers were not particularly successful with seminars, they were just learning how to make cooperative learning groups more uniformly constructive, and there were some problems accommodating studies in foreign languages and the arts. The demarcation between the two programs was too sharp. Students were too isolated in their respective academic studies. It has been recognized that, for students, school is a social as well as an academic experience. Unfortunately, the two programs were set up in opposition. This may not have been the intent but students and their parents felt it and so did teachers. The evaluation process may have accentuated the competitiveness" (p. 133). There is more to learn.

The "bottomline": "These results represent a small sample and only two years' experience, and thus cannot be viewed as conclusive. However, it is clear that the assumption that the traditional daily and yearly schedules are the more effective has been seriously challenged. Responsibility for justification now falls on those who favor the Traditional schedule. **Implementing a Copernican style schedule can be accomplished with the expectation of favorable pedagogical outcomes.**" (p. 134)

Part II

The Experience of Other Schools

The Harvard team concluded that schools implementing a Copernican type schedule could do so with the expectation of favorable pedagogical outcomes. We now turn to the evaluation of experience of other schools that have implemented a Copernican style program. What is their experience? Efforts to answer that question in a reliable manner proved to be quite difficult, primarily because the answer could only come from students and then, only in terms of improved student performance.

STRUCTURING THE EVALUATION OF OTHER COPERNICAN SCHOOLS

The first task to be undertaken in determining the impact of Copernican restructuring is to identify a group of schools that have implemented a Copernican style program. That presented an interesting problem. There is no formal network of Copernican schools. However, the concepts are becoming widely known, particularly among secondary school educators. The substantial dissemination of these concepts has certainly resulted in many schools adopting this structure. However, there is no systematic way of learning of all of them. The information arrives via phone calls and letters. I learned of some implementing districts from members of the audience after making presentations. Two executive teachers from Claremont, Tasmania sent me a copy of several Copernican schedules their staff were considering. I know of a considerable number of schools that have definitely implemented a Copernican schedule and have been advised that there are many more of which I am not aware. In any case, there were implementing schools. The problem would be to find schools that were willing and able to participate in this evaluation.

Implementation varies. Some schools have initiated longer classes but have not reduced the numbers of classes with which teachers and students must deal each day. Other schools have seen the concepts more clearly and have developed programs which implement them more fully. Will different models get different results? It must be reemphasized that changing of the schedule is not an end in itself but rather a means for achieving several important ends. The most important of these are creating significantly more manageable teacher and student workloads and fundamentally strengthening the relationship between teachers and students; all of which is accomplished through a fundamental change in the use of time in the daily and annual schedule. The projected impact on workloads and relationships are the experimental variables that need to be evaluated.

I needed to develop an evaluation plan that could be applied validly to schools using different Copernican schedules. This objective presented problems but also an opportunity. Might it be possible to evaluate the relative effectiveness of different Copernican models?

There were other problems. Most schools initiating a Copernican program have very limited plans for evaluation. What evaluation is being done usually does not address academic outcomes. I needed to develop a common system for evaluating very different schools. Timing was also a problem. Only a few programs had begun implementation by September 1991, and the majority were in their first year of implementation during the 1992-93 school year. There was one important common factor. The questions which these schools relay to me consistently include those addressed above by the Harvard evaluation. The academic questions were the ones most schools found most difficult to address and there was great concern on how to answer skeptics and critics who simply asked: "Show me that students learn more under this proposed new schedule." And in every case, we needed reliable data.

It took a long time and some false starts to structure an evaluation that could meet the above specifications. It is now possible to review the results of changing to a Copernican structure because some of these schools were able to provide reliable evaluative data comparing five measures of student performance during the last year under a traditional structure with student performance during the first year under a Copernican structure. Also, six of these schools shifted "whole school" without changes in curriculum or grading standards from those in the previous year under a traditional structure; and additionally, other than normal turnover, there was no change in the staff. None had major staff development programs which would impair a fair comparison of the results of these two years, or other events which could account for changes in student performance that might be identified through this evaluation.

This format addresses directly the question of whether the schools improved in terms of generally accepted measures of school performance: attendance, retention or dropout rates, suspension rates, and academic performance. Attendance and dropout rates were those reported to state/provincial authorities which ensured reliability. Suspension rates are not required reporting in all states but most schools maintained such records. While schools may differ in their policies and practices concerning suspension, these schools did not differ sharply from their last year under a traditional structure and their first year under a Copernican structure. Academic measures were based on grading as practiced in each school, but in two cases, these school results were buttressed by strong state/provincial testing programs. These measures of mastery will be explained in detail in the context of presenting information concerning these schools.

These seven schools represent a variety of Copernican models. Comparisons between models are based upon the relative change in the year to year comparisons for each school. Each school represented a separate evaluation. Since they used the same evaluative criteria, they also, as a group, test the Harvard evaluators conclusion concerning "pedagogical gain" and shed light on the relative effectiveness of different Copernican models.

The following sections will present the details of this evaluative format for each of the schools, beginning with a measure of the degree to which each school implemented the Copernican Plan. After considering all of the schools evaluations, a composite evaluation is presented under the section called "Copernican Messages."

THE COPERNICAN FACTOR:

The following schools present different versions of a Copernican schedule. This is to be expected since each school had to deal with the organizational and political realities of its school and staff, its community, and its state or provincial regulations in developing its program. However, each school's program targets the two principal Copernican objectives: fundamentally improving the relationships between teachers and students, and creating significantly more manageable workloads for both teachers and students. However, the level of implementation of the Copernican concepts varies significantly.

A good measure of the level of implementation is the sum of the number of classes that a teacher teaches and the number of classes in which a student is enrolled each day. For example, a traditional high school program typically has students taking six classes and teachers teaching five classes per day; the Copernican factor is the sum of the two numbers or 11. The Copernican programs which will be evaluated are presented in ascending order of their respective Copernican factors.

L.V. ROGERS SECONDARY SCHOOL
NELSON, BRITISH COLUMBIA
"THE HORIZONTAL TIMETABLE"

Daily classes per teacher:	2
Daily classes per student:	2
Copernican Factor:	4

The L.V.Rogers Secondary School is a three year secondary school which serves approximately 650 students in Nelson, British Columbia. Nelson is a self contained, middle income community. For many years, L.V.Rogers was rated a good, above average school with a solid program. However, Bill Reid, the principal, was not satisfied. "Concerned at a 28 percent drop out rate—slightly lower than the provincial average—Reid came up with the horizontal timetable idea when he read about the so-called Copernican Plan in Boston."[11]

The standard "timetable" for secondary schools in British Columbia revolves around students enrolling in eight courses at one time. Some schools rotate the periods on five, or six periods per day. The L.V.Rogers traditional schedule provided for four classes to be taught each day, with provisions to rotate the schedule so classes would meet at different times of day and the cycle would be complete in eight days; Students were dealing with eight classes at one time; similarly, teachers, while teaching no more than four classes each day, were dealing with seven classes at a time; assuming an average class size of 25, teacher were dealing with about 175 students, simultaneously. The Copernican Factor for the traditional program at L.V.Rogers was 15.

The Horizontal Timetable, which is shown in Exhibit 3 on the following page, is an excellent example of adapting the Copernican concepts to this particular environment. Each student enrolls in two, 2 1/2 hour classes each day, one in the morning and one in the afternoon. Every week the morning class is shifted to the afternoon and the afternoon class is held in the morning, thus balancing out the negative impact

Exhibit 3
L.V. Rogers Horizontal Timetable

Time	Period	Mon.	Tues.	Wed.	Thurs.	Fri.
7:30 8:30	Seminar One	Choir		Choir		Choir
8:45 11:15	Period One	A	A	A	A	A
11:15 11:45	Tutorial					
11:15 12:15	Seminar Two	Band	Stage Band	Band	Stage Band	
11:45 12:45	Lunch					
12:45 3:15	Period Two	B	B	B	B	B

of after lunch drowsiness and normal weariness. Similarly, teachers teach only two, 2 1/2 hour classes each day. Each class is completed in a single quarter. At the end of four quarters, each student has completed eight classes, as per the provincial requirement, and each teacher has taught seven classes. (For one quarter each year, a teacher teaches only one class.) Please note that the total time allotted to complete a course is roughly the same as was available under the traditional schedule, in contrast to Masconomet's Renaissance Program schedule which allotted about 20% to 25% less time to complete a course than was allotted under the traditional schedule. Also, classes met in a double period (90 minutes) twice during the traditional program's eight day cycle; thus, the L.V.Rogers teaching staff had many years of experience teaching a 90 minute class, an experience shared by very few secondary teachers in the United States. As will be described later, some schools which have adopted the Copernican schedule have moved to 90 minute classes, while L.V.Rogers moved to 150 minute classes.

How have students fared under the horizontal time table? Consider the following evaluative information.

How did students react to this level of concentration?

A 26-item questionnaire was administered during each of the first two quarters of the first year to a random sampling of students, which provided 52 opportunities to respond positively or negatively to the Horizontal Timetable.[12] A five point Likert Scale was used for responses (Strongly Agree, Agree, No Opinion, Disagree, and Strongly Disagree). On none of these 52 responses did 50% or more of the students respond negatively. Seventy percent or more of the students responded positively on

20 of the 52 responses. On only two questions did more than a third of the students respond negatively. The following are the five statements responded to most positively and least positively at the end of two quarters experience with the Horizontal Timetable:

Most positive responses: (Based on "strongly agree" plus "agree" responses on the final administration of the survey at the end of the second quarter.)

"I like completing some of my courses (including final exams) at the end of each quarter rather than completing all eight courses in June."
(94% responded positively)

"I am attending class more often."
(86% responded positively)

"It is easier to prepare for unit tests because I have only two classes"
(83% responded positively)

"The new timetable provides for more extra-help time with teachers."
(80% responded positively)

"There is an increased learning intensity in my courses."
(78% responded positively)

Least positive responses: (Based on "disagree" plus "strongly disagree" responses on the final administration of the survey at the end of the second quarter.)

"Material is presented at a good pace for most students."
(44% responded negatively)

"It is easier to catch up the work missed after I have missed school because of sickness."
(43% responded negatively)

"I feel less confusion and stress in school this year."
(31% responded negatively)

"The horizontal timetable allows for more participation in extracurricular activities."
(24% responded negatively)

"The absence of bells is good."
(23% responded negatively)

These responses are remarkably positive and clearly show that the students viewed the program as beneficial to them and that they are able to work well with two, two and a half hour courses per day on a quarter basis.

How did teachers respond to this level of concentration?

A 24-item questionnaire was administered to the faculty during each of the first two quarters; this allowed each teacher a total of 48 responses.[13] Again, a five point Likert Scale was used for responses (Strongly Agree, Agree, No Opinion, Disagree, and Strongly Disagree. On only one of these 48 responses did more than 50% of the staff respond negatively. Seventy percent or more of the teachers responded positively on 20 of these 48 comparisons.

These are the five questions responded to most positively and least positively:

Most positive responses: (Based on "strongly agree" plus "agree" responses on the final administration of the survey at the end of the second quarter.)

"The absence of bells is good."
(91% responded positively)

"Less class time is disrupted by other activities."
(88% responded positively)

"The new timetable is meeting the student's educational needs."
(77% responded positively)

"The new timetable provides for more extra help time with students."
(77% responded positively)

"I am able to make better use of class time."
(74% responded positively)

Least positive responses: (Based on "disagree" plus "strongly disagree" responses on the final administration of the survey at the end of the second quarter.)

"I have time to interact with my peers."
(51% responded negatively.)

"I feel less stressed because of the new timetable."
(40% responded negatively)

"Less time is spent on non-teaching duties (paperwork)."
(37% responded negatively)

"I am more able to complete the curricular requirements on schedule."
(21% responded negatively)

"The new timetable has enhanced my teaching."
(15% responded negatively)

The great majority of the teaching staff responded very positively to the Horizontal Timetable.

ATTENDANCE

Principal Bill Reid, in a letter to the author, reported: "—overall attendance has improved by 6% while tardiness has decrease by 10%."[14] Attendance rates went from about 90% to 95%.

SUSPENSIONS

L.V.Rogers Secondary is an orderly school and does not have an unusually high level of disciplinary problems. Two out of three students complete their three years without a disciplinary note in their files. It should be noted that enrollments were 9% higher in 1991-92 (666) than in 1990-91 (610), and the number of disciplinary problems would normally have increased somewhat proportionately. However, this increase did not occur. Student conduct made important improvements in the first year under the Horizontal Timetable.

A comparison of the number of students seen by an administrator for disciplinary reasons in the 1990-91 school year, the year preceding the Horizontal Timetable, and the 1991-92 school year, the first year under the Horizontal time table, finds a reduction of about 20%.[15] Suspensions dropped approximately 25% in the first year under the Horizontal Timetable.[16]

This substantial reduction in disciplinary problems reflects the overall improvement in school climate as a result of the Copernican schedule. Approximately 2/3rds of the teachers agreed with the statement: "I know more about my students as individuals." Students responded similarly to these statements: "My teachers know more about me as an individual" and "I am enjoying school more this year". The relationships between teachers and students significantly improved, and to the extent that occurs, discipline problems should decrease; and they did.

DROPOUT RATE/RETENTION

Bill Reid, principal of L.V.Rogers Secondary School, made the following observations when he was justifying the need to shift to a Horizontal Timetable: "Our school is as good as any in the province, and better than many. Our dropout rate is low, and our government (provincial) exams results are fine. Despite this, we are only graduating 73% to 75% of our students. One in four grade 12's does not finish in June." Clearly, retention of students was a major objective in proposing the Horizontal Timetable.

One might be confused by the above statement. How can dropout rates be low when only 75% of those enrolling as 12th grade students actually graduate? In British Columbia, drop outs are those who leave school before the end of the school year (not to be confused with transfers.) But many 12th grade students are unable to complete enough courses satisfactorily to earn a diploma. The provincial exams, which represent 40% of a student's final grade in a course, can result in many more students not graduating.

There is no formal report on the number of students who return the following year after failing to graduate, primarily because the Province does not require reporting of this information. However, in the judgment of a number of administrators, a very small percentage of these students return. Thus, the failure to graduate is equivalent to a dropout.

It should be noted that enrollments increased from 610 in 1990-91 to 666 students in 1991-92, the first year under the Horizontal Timetable, an increase of 9%, which is unusual in a stable community. Although specific numbers were not available, some of this increase was reported to be caused not by new students but by a return of those students who had not graduated. The new schedule would allow them to complete one or two courses in one quarter rather than having to attend class for an entire year. The return of dropouts is a converse measure of retention under the Horizontal Timetable.

As Principal Reid stated, the dropout rate at L.V.Rogers is low; it was 2.5% in both the 1990-91 and 1991-92 school years. However, the percentage of students failing to graduate dropped from 27% (73% graduating) in 1990-91 to about 10% (90% graduating) in 1991-92, a 63% reduction in the proportion of students not graduating.[17] This sharp reduction in the percentage of students failing to graduate is consistent with the evaluative information presented above and the academic results presented in the next section.

ACADEMICS

Before considering specific academic analyses, some observations concerning the instructional program are necessary to put this information in proper context. Please note that the movement to the Horizontal Timetable, to two 2 1/2 hour classes per day, was not accompanied by a change in the organization of nor the content of the curriculum. There were no new academic standards introduced to impact on grades. Teachers taught what they had taught in previous years only under a Copernican schedule. The school was able to pay teachers to work some over the summer to reconfigure their courses for the 2 1/2 hour classes but there was no major staff development program. The only change, and it was a major change, was the change in the schedule and the impact of that change on teachers and students.

There are several measures of the impact on academic performance of the Horizontal Timetable; in each case, comparisons will be made with the students' performances in 1990-91, the year prior to initiating the Horizontal Timetable and the last year under a traditional schedule, and their performances in 1991-92, the first year under the Horizontal Timetable.

GRADES EARNED

Exhibit 4, found on the following page, presents a comparison of the distribution of final grades earned by L.V.Rogers' students in the 1990-91 and 1991-92 school years. This distribution includes all final grades in all subjects for the entire year. This Exhibit shows a major improvement in grades under the Horizontal Timetable. The percentage of "A"s doubled; the percentage of "F"s was halved. Overall, statistically, this improvement is at the .0001 level of significance. Please note carefully that this level of significance means that if the Copernican change did not actually have some impact on the academic success of students, the odds on getting this result by chance are less than one chance in 10,000. In a profession where one chance in 20 is considered significant, this is an immensely impressive academic outcome.

MASTERY OF COURSE CONTENT

The bottom line on Exhibit 4 is an estimate that there was a 10% increase in actual mastery of course content in 1991-92 as a result of the introduction of the Horizontal Timetable. How can this statement be supported when very few high schools, and none presented in this book, would claim to be utilizing mastery learning or outcomes based education. Since this type of analysis will be used to evaluate academic mastery for other high schools presented later in this book, let us now review the basis for determining mastery in some detail.

BASIS FOR THIS ANALYSIS

There was no change in curriculum or grading standards when L.V.Rogers Secondary School shifted to the Horizontal Timetable. In L.V.Rogers, there will usually be some shift in teaching assignments from year to year, some change in staff and students, but these are not systemic changes nor different from those which will occur from year to year in virtually all high schools. The significant variable is the Copernican change, the Horizontal Timetable.

Exhibit 4
An Estimate of Mastery of Course Content
Based Upon an Analysis of Grade Earned at L.V. Rogers Secondary School, Nelson, British Columbia, 1990–91 & 1991–92

Grades Earned	Traditional 1991 No.	Traditional 1991 %	Copernican 1992 No.	Copernican 1992 %	Diff. %	Mastery est. in %	Avg. Percent of Mastery 1991	Avg. Percent of Mastery 1992
A	355	9%	726	19%	105%	95%	33725	68970
B	960	25%	1385	37%	44%	85%	81600	117725
C+	645	17%	738	20%	14%	77%	49665	56826
C	668	18%	558	15%	−16%	72%	48096	40176
P	838	22%	521	14%	−38%	63%	52794	32823
F	301	8%	150	4%	−50%	50%	15050	7500

Total A – F:	3767		4078				280930	324020
Total A – P:	3466		3928		Est. % Mastered		74.58%	79.46%
Enrollment	610		666		Est. Incr. in Mastery			6.5%
Courses/Student	5.68		5.90		X2 Test: P < 0.0001 (sig.)			
% Increase	—		3.8%					

Est. Total Increase in Mastery: 10%
Higher Grades and Increases
in Courses Completed.*

° Assumptions upon which this estimate is based:
  1. That higher grades represent a higher level of mastery. The percentages used (95% for A's, etc.) are commonly used to define these grades and represent a valid standard.
  2. That the successful completion of a larger number of courses of study represents a greater mastery of course material by a student.

Sources: L.V. Rogers Secondary School records regarding distribution of grades and enrollments for 1990–91 and 1991–92.

The grades shown on Exhibit 4 represent all of the grades earned by all of the students. It is not a sampling of the students, or perhaps it could be described as a 100% sample. Applying a chi square analysis to these grades finds that the change in the distribution of grades from 1990-91 to 1991-92 is significant at the .0001 level. As stated above, this is a very high level of significance.

These estimates of mastery are based upon two premises, which we should examine carefully. The first premise is that when a teacher awards an "A", this is evidence that a student has mastered more of the course objectives than another student who received a "B"; and that a "B" grade indicates greater mastery than a "C", and a "C" is evidence of greater mastery than a "D". While it is unlikely that any one will disagree with this logic, what is a reasonable basis for comparing the levels of mastery associated with these different grades?

There is a reasonable answer to the above question. There is general acceptance of the position that an "A" is equated with "90% or more mastery of the objectives and/or performance requirements of a course of study; similarly, a "B" is equated with an 80% to 89% level of mastery; a "C" is equated at 70% to 79%; a "D" with 60% to 69%; and "F"'s are equated with less than 60% and, probably incorrectly, with so little mastery that no credit is given.[18] There is an inherent question when dealing with these concepts. What is 70% in an art program as compared with 70% in a math program? But Art and Math teachers do have objectives which they wish their students to achieve, and each discipline has systematic approaches to assessing the degree to which a student masters these objectives.

In Exhibit 4, the grades awarded during the year prior to initiation of the Horizontal Timetable and the grades earned in the first year under the Horizontal Timetable are weighted and averaged based on the estimates of mastery articulated above. These significantly higher grades account for an increase in mastery of about 6.5%. Please note that if this analysis were done using the traditional 4 point grade scale, the weighting commonly used to determine grade point averages and usually utilized in research comparing grades, the increase would be 17.3%. Thus this measure of mastery is more conservative but much more valid.

The other measure of mastery is in the average number of courses each student completes with a passing grade in a year. It is reasonable to believe that a student has mastered more course content if he or she completes, satisfactorily, a larger number of courses in a year. The reductions in failure rates as well as students completing more courses are valid measures of the relative levels of mastery in the two years. In the case of L.V.Rogers Secondary School, the average student completed 3.8% more courses satisfactorily than did students in the previous year under the traditional schedule. This increase was totally a result of the precipitous reduction in failure rates. Please note that L.V.Rogers students enrolled in eight classes per year under both the traditional schedule and the Horizontal Timetable, so all of their improvements in mastery were based on higher grades and fewer failures. This is different from the other schools which will be reported later, because these other schools' Copernican schedules offer opportunities to enroll in more courses per year than is possible under their respective traditional schedules.

Thus 11%, the sum of these two measures, provides a valid comparison of the increased mastery of course content achieved by students at L.V.Rogers Secondary School in the first year under the Horizontal Timetable.

PROVINCIAL TWELFTH GRADE EXAMS

There is always a concern that the improvements cited above, could reflect grade escalation on the part of a group of teachers, the majority of whom voted to try the Horizontal Timetable and who, subliminally, might be a bit less than objective in awarding grades in order to justify their decision. Fortunately, the Province of British Columbia administers a series of examinations to all twelfth grade students in the province. These are "high stakes" examinations, because they represent 40% of a students final grade in the course. These exams are not controlled locally, and thus the performance of the L.V.Rogers students on these exams will be free of the possibility of grade escalation. How did the L.V.Rogers students perform on the provincial examinations during the first year under the Horizontal Timetable as compared to their performance in the previous year under a traditional structure?

Exhibit 5, found on the following page, makes two comparisons concerning the failure rates on the provincial exams. The first comparison finds that in 1990-91, under a traditional schedule, L.V.Rogers had fewer failures than did the province as a whole in 6 of 9 comparisons; the average difference was 4%. However, in 1991-92, under the Horizontal Timetable, L.V.Rogers had fewer failures than the province as a whole in all 10 of 10 comparisons, and the average difference was 7%.

Exhibit 5 also compares the 1990-91 and 1991-92 failure rates of L.V.Rogers students on the provincial exams. Five of nine comparisons favor the 1991-92 performance. The average difference in these five comparisons was 14% while the average difference in the tests favoring the traditional year was 2%.

Exhibit 6 (page 26), makes a similar comparison of the percentage of "A"s earned on the provincial examinations and the numbers of students qualifying for provincial scholarships. L.V.Rogers students exceeded the provincial average of "A" grades in only 3 of 9 comparisons on the 1990-91 provincial examinations; but in 1991-92, L.V.Rogers students exceeded the provincial average in 7 of 10 comparisons. Also, the L.V.Rogers percentage of "A"s in 1991-92 exceeded those earned in 1990-91 in 7 of 9 comparisons. The average difference was 9%.

The provincial examinations are also important because they are the basis for awarding scholarships to students. The provincial exams have scaled scores, similar to the SAT (e.g. range of 200 to 800). Any student who can earn a total of 1700 on any three of the provincial examinations will receive a $1000 scholarship. Prior to 1991-92, the largest number of provincial scholarships earned in any year by L.V.Rogers students was 6. The average number of scholarships awarded L.V.Rogers students for the last four years under the traditional schedule was 3.5. In 1991-92, the first year under the Horizontal Timetable, L.V. Rogers students were awarded 16 scholarships, an increase of approximately 400%. (It should be noted that 16 scholarships also were awarded the second year under the Horizontal Timetable.)

Exhibit 5
L.V. Rogers High School, Nelson, British Columbia
Provincial Exams: Failure Rates

| Subject | 1991–92 Copernican | | 1990–91 Traditional | |
	Provincial % F's	LV Rogers % F's	Provincial % F's	LV Rogers % F's
Biology 12	17.52%	11.57%	18.50%	29.50%
Chemistry 12	11.50%	1.81%	13.20%	0.00%
Communic. 12	15.24%	6.81%	9.20%	5.60%
English 12	8.74%	3.50%	7.80%	3.80%
English Lit. 12	11.59%	0.00%	No Test	No Test
French 12	9.35%	0.00%	0.70%	0.00%
Geography 12	10.71%	7.69%	10.30%	5.90%
History 12	14.37%	7.89%	11.50%	8.70%
Mathematics 12	16.90%	7.04%	16.10%	42.90%
Physics 12	15.65%	8.82%	17.00%	23.10%

Summary:

In 1990–91, Rogers had fewer failures than did the Province in 6 of 9 comparisons; the average difference was 4%. In 1991–92, Rogers had fewer failures in 10 of 10 comparisons; the average difference was 7%.

Rogers had fewer failures in 1991–92 than in 1990–91 in 5 of 9 comparisons; the average reduction was 14%. Differences favoring the traditional year averaged 2%.

Sources: Province of British Columbia Ministry of Education Report on Grade 12 Examinations 1990–91 and 1991–92.

SUMMATION

The L.V.Rogers Secondary School is a good school that decided it must become much better. They initiated the Horizontal Timetable in order to establish a structure that would accommodate change and pedagogical improvements. The Horizontal Timetable reduces the Copernican factor from 15 to 4, which is a major change, a Copernican change. The surveys of students and teachers clearly show that this major change in the schedule resulted in much better relationships between teachers and students and more manageable workloads for both teachers and students, which are the objectives sought in making this change. Student attendance improved and discipline problems declined sharply. The academic evaluations are remarkably positive and are statistically significant at an extraordinarily high level of confidence. Students mastered about 11% more course material. There were a number of students who had failed to graduate who returned because the new schedule was more flexible and accommodated their needs. Finally, the school was able to graduate 90% of its 12th grade students versus only about 75% in previous years. And the higher performing students performed even better under the Horizontal timetable. The benefits were school-wide rather than for only one group of students. Once again, nothing has happened in education until it happens to a student. All of these gains are a result of the impact of the new structure on students, and the improvements are truly Copernican.

Exhibit 6
L.V. Rogers High School, Nelson, British Columbia
Provincial Exams: Percentage of A's/Scholarships

| Subject | 1991–92 Copernican | | 1990–91 Traditional | |
	Provincial % A's	LV Rogers % A's	Provincial % A's	LV Rogers % A's
Biology 12	11.06%	9.47%	10.30%	2.60%
Chemistry 12	19.00%	29.09%	16.50%	22.70%
Communic. 12	3.40%	4.54%	3.90%	5.60%
English 12	9.57%	13.00%	9.00%	6.10%
English Lit. 12	11.38%	15.38%	No Test	No Test
French 12	12.48%	13.63%	13.80%	30.00%
Geography 12	5.36%	5.12%	6.10%	0.00%
History 12	5.49%	18.42%	7.60%	0.00%
Mathematics 12	14.21%	9.85%	12.50%	4.80%
Physics 12	21.36%	20.58%	19.70%	7.70%

Recapitulation:

In 1990–91, Rogers exceeded the Provincial scores in only 3 of 9 comparisons; in 1991–92, Rogers exceeded the Provincial scores in 7 of 10 comparisons.

Rogers' percentages in 1991–92 exceeded those of 1990–91 in 7 of 9 comparisons.

Number Qualifying for Provincial Scholarships

Average for the last four years:*	Copernican 1991–92:
3.5	16

° Rogers previous high was 6.

A WORD FROM THE SCHOOL

The research on more effective schools shows clearly that leadership is a key ingredient in successful schools. L.V.Rogers Secondary School's principal, Bill Reid, provided excellent leadership, packaged in a firm, focused and friendly style. The following statement from Bill adds an important perspective concerning the development of the Horizontal Time Table.

"The Horizontal Timetable had a successful debut at L.V. Rogers. A survey by the School Board at the end of the first year showed that only seven per cent of the parents and students wanted to switch back to a linear system.

"A variety of academic records were set in the school:

- highest number of Ministry Scholarships in a year at 16. The previous high was six.
- highest number of qualifying scores on government exams.
- highest number of students achieving Honor Roll status.
- highest passing rate in most individual courses.
- highest graduation rate.

"The failure rates in most courses in the school came down dramatically. In Science 10, for example, the failure rate dropped to three per cent from 20%. This resulted in more students selecting an academic science class for their grade 11 year. Many students took full advantage of the spiralling math curriculum (Introductory Math 11 to Math 11 to Math 12). There is a tremendous desire in students to succeed in the academic courses.

"Those students who did fail often took advantage of the opportunity to repeat a critical course such as Social Studies 11. We also experienced an increase in the selection of self-directed learning as students designed a curriculum around their needs and interests.

"People who visited the school commented frequently on the relaxed but focused academic atmosphere. We expected some improvement in school climate, but were very pleasantly surprised by the extent of the change. We had anticipated a similar or slightly reduced number of discipline problems and were pleased to see a major reduction.

"Inservice for teachers is important. We were able to allocate some money so teachers could work in the summer reconfiguring their courses for the extended time blocks. We could have used some professional development in the school year to improve our techniques and take full advantage of the long periods. It is also important that equipment in specialty areas be well kept and operational. In a linear system we could get away with equipment being broken for a week. On this timetable it needs to be fixed as soon as possible.

"We reported to parents eight times a year and held parent interviews after the midterm report. This was not effective in the case of parents with a child in difficulty and we are considering some alternatives. Teachers know the students quite well by the end of the first two weeks of a course and we will probably rely more on teachers phoning parents when they see a problem developing.

"In building our timetable, we start from scratch every year, using a conflict matrix to create the best possible situation for the greatest number of students. We were able to accommodate most teacher requests for the placement of their courses and preparation blocks. We pay close attention to the placement of courses so that students can get the full benefit from the flexibility of the timetable. For example, Introductory Math 11 is timetabled before Math 11. Biology 11, which focuses on plants is programmed for the first and fourth quarters to take advantage of the weather. French 11 is programmed before French 12. Students are given a choice of taking a winter or summer season Physical Education class.

"In switching timetables we listened to a lot of people give us reasons it would not work. Students could not concentrate for over two hours. Students would forget from one year to the next. A school needs bells to operate. Teachers cannot change to accommodate the long periods. Students would not be ready for university. Special needs students would suffer. But we did it, and all those excuses have fallen by the wayside.

"The timetable does work; kids and teachers like the timetable. I think that every school should study what we are doing as an option for consideration. If it helps kids, it deserves a try."

W. Reid, Principal
L. V. Rogers Secondary School
Nelson, British Columbia

CHELSEA HIGH SCHOOL
CHELSEA, MASSACHUSETTS
THE TRIMESTER PROGRAM

Daily classes per teacher:	2
Daily classes per student:	3
Copernican Factor:	5

Chelsea is a small city comprising three square miles which borders Boston on the north. It was once a fairly affluent suburb, but over the last half century most of the affluence has left, the town has not been able to develop a strong economic base, and Chelsea is now a microcosm of our nation's most difficult urban problems.

Chelsea's School Committee faced all the challenges of a problem plagued, urban school system. The schools were "long" on problems and "short" on funds. Then, in 1989, the Chelsea School Committee made a proposal which, in the true sense of the word, was unique. The idea really came from the president of Boston University, John Silber. Dr. Silber may well be the major critic of the Boston Public Schools; and he has considerable competition for that recognition. Dr. Silber had on a number of occasions stated that he would arrange for Boston University to manage the Boston schools on a contract basis, and that if this were done, the children of Boston would be much better educated. Dr. Silber was serious about his proposal, but there was no way to implement it, politically. The Chelsea School Committee indicated that it would consider such a proposal. Months later, after much debate and passage of special authorizing legislation by the State Legislature, the deal was completed. Chelsea's schools would be managed by a team established via the Boston University School of Education.

Chelsea is, in at least one aspect, a much more difficult problem than Boston. While Boston has a high per pupil cost and a strong tax base, Chelsea was one of the poorest districts in the state. Over 60% of Chelsea's school enrollments are minorities. Chelsea High School has the problems that characterize a tough urban high school, eg: the school has for many years had the highest dropout rate in the Commonwealth, which is above 50%. The economy in Massachusetts, and for that matter in the entire Northeast, was in deep trouble in fiscal year 1990-91, and the State's funding for schools suffered seriously. All schools faced a tough 1991-92 school year. But a district such as Chelsea, which depended very heavily upon state funding, was in particular trouble. In late June of 1991, I received a call from a member of the B.U. Management Team who was acquainted with the Copernican Plan, and was asked to donate a day to work with the principal and two assistant principals of Chelsea High School to see if the Copernican approach might help alleviate a very difficult problem.

The problem was as follows. Because of the loss of funding, the Chelsea schools were going to have to cut staff. The Management Team had decided, on a priority basis, to retain most of its early childhood program pretty much intact, which meant that the secondary program would have to bear a disproportionate share of the cuts. As a result, the high school administration had to figure out how best to operate after a cut in its teaching staff of about 40%. (It actually turned out to be about 35%.) Also, because of problems with the teachers' contractual language, every teacher—K through 12—was "riffed"; given notice of termination. (Riffed stands for "reduction in force".) The number of teachers that could be retained, that is rehired, would be determined later after programatic questions were determined and some of the funding problems clarified. Furthermore, the town's finances were in such a sorry state that the state government was seriously considering placing the city under a receivership. This was done later that summer. The problem, simply put, was how to organize a tough, urban high school with 40% less staff so that most of the about 850 students would have an education that would not be too much less adequate than was the case the previous year. Given these circumstances, this was indeed a challenge.

It was a productive day. The principal and the two assistant principals grasped the basic concepts rather well. With each teacher teaching six classes per year, they could offset about 20% of the loss of staff and could retain more of the curriculum. Class sizes would still be large, but most would be manageable, as manageable had been defined over the years at Chelsea.

But the purpose of restructuring the schedule was to create better relationships between teachers and students, and also more manageable workloads for both teachers and students. The problem was that school was out. They had no way to work with their teachers; in fact they were not even certain which teachers would be on their teaching staff the following September, since all teachers had been "pink slipped". If they made this move, there would not be time for staff involvement, staff development, and no way in which to let the parents and students know what was happening and why. To schedule traditionally or move to a Copernican schedule? This was the decision that the principal had to make. I was leaving shortly for a fairly active summer. We agreed to get together when I returned at the end of July.

When I returned, I had a message to call Chelsea. Elsa Wasserman, Chelsea High School's principal, told me that they had decided to implement a Copernican schedule, which they called the Trimester. The Trimester schedule is shown in Exhibit 7, which is found on the following page. Students would take three, 95 minute classes each day for a trimester; thus they could enroll in nine classes per year. Teachers would teach two classes per day; in three trimesters, they would teach six classes. But they had a few problems. They had to reschedule the entire high school. Students had selected courses on the assumption of a seven period day; they now had nine periods. They were just now getting the decision on who would be rehired as teachers, which had some impact on what could be offered. It is difficult to describe the level of pressure on those three administrators at that time. Based on considerable experience in pressure situations, the principal was looking forward to a great deal of heat. If she had decided to follow a traditional schedule, she had a guaranteed disaster, but she would not be the one who would be blamed for the situation. Her decision was to gamble for a better program for the students. It was a long shot, based upon the processes the conventional wisdom of the profession describes as absolutely necessary to successfully change a school. If this restructuring did not result in at least as good a program as the previous year, she would carry most of the blame. However, it was helpful that the superintendent, Peter Greer—an experienced and capable administrator who left his position as Dean of the Boston University School of Education to be the superintendent at Chelsea—supported the decision.

But the heat was on. The teacher union president was reportedly very angry. The union roundly criticized the decision to go to a Trimester program which had been terminated at Masconomet. The union also issued a statement condemning the decision. But the anger was to be expected. One person asked how I could have let them make this move; "It will be a disaster". My response was: "If it is a disaster, how would you be able to tell the difference considering the large cut in teaching staff?" While it was not my decision, it was the decision I would have made. As school prepared to open, I was asked to arrange for two teachers who had taught in the

Exhibit 7

Chelsea High School Trimester Program: Typical Student's Schedule

Trimester I	Trimester II	Trimester III
Algebra I	Graphic Art	Biology
History	Physical Education	Geometry
Homeroom, Study, Band, Chorus, Drama or Other Full Year Courses		
Lunch ---		
English	Spanish I	Spanish II

Renaissance Program to speak to the Chelsea staff as part of the preschool program. They did a great job. However, the preschool program provided during the three preschool days was all the staff development Chelsea teachers had when they began teaching in the Trimester Program.

What was the result of this "gutsie" and controversial decision? As the program began, I received phone calls fairly regularly from the principal and two assistant principals, asking questions concerning problems encountered or questions asked of them. But then the concerns declined. One day, Andre Ravenelle, one of the assistant principals, commented that attendance was averaging about 85%. Attendance the previous year was 77% and 85% was about the highest it reached on any day the previous year. Near the end of September, after a long telephone discussion with Ron Toleos, the other assistant principal, concerning some questions, I asked how the school was faring. His reply was memorable: The disciplinary problems had dropped off remarkably. The school climate had basically changed. Not long after this, I arrived home late and found a very long message on my answering machine from the principal, Elsa Wasserman. She had been withholding judgment and concentrating on visiting classrooms to see what was happening. It was working, not 100%, but things were changing and the changes were very positive. Later Andre Ravenelle told me that "our concentration has shifted from the corridors to the classrooms", a reference to the major reduction in disciplinary problems, which seemed to be concentrated in the passing times between classes.

The majority of Chelsea High School teachers were trying to make use of the longer, 95 minute class and were having some success, although the criticisms did continue. The administration was trying to help them. Some staff still relied on lectures, but instructional alternatives were surfacing more and more. And most important, teachers were talking to and working with students on a regular, more personal basis. Research has consistently identified motivation as the beginning of learning, and teachers were using their increased, in depth contact with students to motivate them.

The following is the more formal evaluation of Chelsea's first year under the Trimester:

ATTENDANCE

Attendance increased from 77% to 81.3%, an increase of about 6% during the first year.[19] This improvement was helped by a systematic telephoning of parents of absent students which was initiated that year, but the administrators believed the Trimester program was the major factor because it caused more students to want to be in school. They noted the improved attendance was evident in the first month of school.

SUSPENSIONS

Suspensions declined about 75% in the first year of the Trimester. Exhibit 8, shown on the following page, compares the suspensions reported on state reports for 1990-91, the year preceding the initiation of the Trimester, and 1991-92, the first year of the Trimester. It should be noted that Chelsea High School had a very high suspension rate. The improvement in climate, which was reported so graphically by the administrators during the first month under the Trimester, continued throughout the year. The "out of school" suspensions dropped 59%. "In-school" suspensions were simply phased out; the assistant principals said that when a problem occurred, it usually was with only one of the student's three teachers. A student would stay out of class for a day or two, but continued in the other classes.

Guidance and the assistant principals were always able to work out these problems and return the students to class . They credit the teachers' significantly increased ability to deal directly with students as the reason for this improvement.

DROPOUT RATES/RETENTION

Dropout rates declined from 13.3% to 8.5% in the first year of the Trimester, a decline of about 36% in one year.[20] This information is shown in detail in Exhibit 9, which follows Exhibit 8. That is a remarkable reduction. What changed?

The Chelsea staff found that one of the major reasons for the reduction in dropouts was that in effect, school started three times each year, at the beginning of each trimester, rather than just once a year in September as is the case under the traditional schedule. This change was particularly important to Chelsea High School since the school dealt with a major transient population. Large numbers of students leave each year and are replaced by other students. These students are arriving throughout the year and the school had never been able to help them "catch up" in the year long classes. The teachers didn't have the time. This inability to provide a productive program where the new students could "fit in" created disciplinary problems and resulted in dropouts. Under the Trimester, a student could start with three

Exhibit 8

A Comparison of the Rates of Suspension at Chelsea High School
1990–91 and 1991–92

	1990–91 Traditional	1991–92 Copernican
Enrollment October 1 Grades 9 – 12	839	835
Suspensions:		
In-School:	214	–0–
Out of School:	337	138
Total:	551	138
As a Percent of Enrollment	65.7%	16.5%
Suspensions declined about 75% during the first year of the trimester.		

Sources: 1990–91 and 1991–92 Chapter 188, Massachusetts State Reports.

new classes in December and again in March. This is an advantage in any school but it is particularly important in an urban high school. Similarly, if a student failed a course and wished to retake it, or needed to complete two levels of a subject in one year, it was relatively easy to schedule under the Trimester. Students who are experiencing academic success and feel they are known by the teachers and are part of the class are far less likely to drop out.

Exhibit 9

A Comparison of the Dropout Rates at Chelsea High School
1990–91 and 1991–92

	1990–91 Traditional	1991–92 Copernican
Enrollment October 1 Grades 9 – 12	839	835
Number of Dropouts	112	71
Percent	13.3%	8.5%
The dropout rate declined about 36% during the first year of the trimester.		

Sources: 1990–91 and 1991–92 Chapter 188, Massachusetts State Reports.

To what extent is this improvement the result of moving to the Trimester, a Copernican schedule, as compared to other in-school factors? After all, this school was now being administered by a prestigious school of education. A number of substantial grants had been obtained and some impacted the high school. A good question. What else changed at Chelsea High School between the 1990-91 and 1991-92 school years?[21]

> Chelsea's dropout rates in the three years before Boston University began administering the Chelsea schools were 17.1% in 1986-87, 16.6% in 1987-88, and 17.6% in 1988-89;[22] a 17.1% average dropout rate. It should be noted that in 1989-90, the first year under Boston University, the dropout rate increased to 20.1%, a 15% increase. The dropout rate then declined to 13.3% in 1990-91. The dropout rate ranged above and below the previous three year average, but the 13.3% rate indicates that the efforts to keep at-risk students in school were having some success.

> In 1990-91, Chelsea High School had two professional staff dedicated to reducing dropout rates. This staff was lost in 1991-92, the first year under the Trimester.

> In 1990-91, the school had funded an alternative program, called the Voyager Program, that dealt with about 20 to 25 of the most difficult students. The following year, 1991-92, the huge cut in the high school staff eliminated the Voyager program. However, a new grant allowed a similar program called Pathways to be initiated. Pathways serviced about the same number of students during the first year of the Trimester.

> In 1991-92, Chelsea received a second grant to support a program called "Dreams and Plans". The grant was received after school began. As part of the program, it funded two Hispanic counsellors. However, the first counsellor was employed in November, the director of the program was employed in December, and the second counsellor was employed in January. Guidance and the assistant principals were always able to work out these problems and return the students to class. Certainly, Chelsea's administrators are pleased to have this program. However, because of the late implementation, the administrators did not believe this program accounted for much if any of this improvement during the first year.

> Chelsea's 9th grade team, which dealt with the problems of the freshman class during 1990-91, was terminated in 1991-92 due to loss of funding.

The net difference between the year prior to initiation of the Trimester and the first year under the Trimester was the loss of two staff dedicated to dropout prevention, the loss of a 9th grade team, and the impact of losing over a third of the teaching staff. This is a significant loss of resources. These in-school changes resulted in substantially reduced resources and thus it doesn't appear possible that they could account for this major reduction in suspensions and drop outs; these improvements occurred in spite of these losses.

Are there other factors to be considered to put these major improvements in better perspective? Consider the following:

An analysis of the impact of dropout prevention grants on dropout rates in Massachusetts found that dropout rates "for urban schools targeted by grants declined from 9.4% in 1988 to 8.4% in 1991", a total reduction of 11% over a three year period.[23] In comparison, Chelsea's 36% improvement in one year is remarkable.

Chelsea's 36% reduction in its dropout rate was the median reduction in dropouts among the seven schools included in this research. That three other high schools had even better results than did Chelsea in their first year under a Copernican schedule, lends very strong support to the change in structure as the cause of these improvements. This will be discussed in more detail later in this book.

This information strongly supports the position that the Copernican change in the structure fostered improved relations between teachers and students and resulted in improved student conduct and fewer dropouts.

ACADEMICS/MASTERY

Academic improvements are the "bottom line" in education. What was the impact of the Trimester on student learning, on mastery of the curriculum? Exhibit 10, which is found on the following page, shows that grades improved very significantly and that students probably mastered about 46% more than they did the previous year under the traditional structure. That is quite a claim! What are the supporting facts?

Exhibit 10 presents an estimate of the change in mastery of course content at Chelsea High School in 1991-92, the first year of the Trimester, with that achieved in 1990-91, the year preceding the initiation of the Trimester. This is the same format and logic presented and explained previously in evaluating academic gains at the L.V.Rogers Secondary School. The assumption underlying this estimate is that higher grades and the successful completion of more courses represent valid measures of increased mastery of course content.

Exhibit 10 shows that higher grades reflected a 0.4% increase in mastery. The percentage of A's increased by 25%, a major increase. However, the increase in A's seems to have come from students who formerly earned B's and C's. The 7% increase in F's is very different from the 50% reduction in F's at L.V.Rogers High School (Exhibit 4) and the reductions which will be presented later in considering other schools. Chelsea High School's classroom effectiveness, as measured by grades awarded by teachers, was about the same in both years. However, it should be observed that the reduction in the number of dropouts may account for some of the lower grades, since potential dropouts aren't usually higher performing students.

The major improvement in mastery came from the number of courses students were able to complete successfully. Exhibit 10 shows that the average student successfully completed 4.02 courses in 1990-91; the average student successfully completed 5.85 courses in 1991-92 under the Trimester, a 45.6 percent increase. In terms of student success, this difference is the difference between graduating in four

Exhibit 10

An Estimate of Mastery of Course Content

Based Upon an Analysis of Grades Earned at Chelsea High School, Chelsea, Massachusetts, 1990–91 & 1991–92

Grades Earned	Traditional 1991 No.	%	Copernican 1992 No.	%	Diff. %	Mastery est. in %	Avg. Percent of Mastery 1991	1992
A	625	14%	1154	18%	25%	95%	59375	109630
B	827	19%	1145	18%	–6%	85%	70295	97325
C	735	17%	904	14%	–17%	75%	55125	67800
D	523	12%	654	10%	–16%	65%	33995	42510
Satis.	662	15%	1029	16%	5%	70%	46340	72030
F+Unsatis.	965	22%	1535	24%	7%	50%	48250	76750
Total	4337		6421				313380	466045
Total A – Satis.	3372		4886		Est. % Mastered		72.26	72.58
Enrollment	839		835		Est. Incr. in Mastery			0.4%
Courses/Student	4.019		5.85		X2 Test: P < 0.0001 (sig.)			
% Increase	—		45.6%					
Est. Total Increase in Mastery from both Improved Grades and Increase in Courses Completed.*	46%							

° Assumptions upon which this estimate is based:

  1. That higher grades represent a higher level of mastery. The percentages used (95% for A's, etc.) are commonly used to define these grades and represent a valid standard.
  2. That the successful completion of a larger number of courses of study represents a greater mastery of course material by a student.

Sources: Chelsea High School records regarding distribution of grades and enrollments for 1990–91 and 1991–92.

years or failing to graduate. Specifically, a student must successfully complete five, full credit courses each year to graduate at Chelsea in four years. (5 courses @ 5 credits each for four years for 100 credits) Under the Trimester, they easily meet this requirement; under the traditional schedule, the average student was 20% short of the required credits. The successful course completion by Chelsea students under the Trimester correlates with the significant reduction in dropouts.

SUMMARY

The decision of Boston University to undertake the administration of the troubled Chelsea schools was a landmark decision in the history of American education. It should be noted that members of the Boston University Management Team initiated the action which resulted in bringing the Copernican Trimester Plan to Chelsea High School. Since Boston University has been able to attract other programs to Chelsea High School, it is necessary to consider the impact of programs other than the Copernican Plan in accounting for these gains; and this question was addressed in the preceding sections. The initiation of the Trimester Schedule was the only change that was significant in impact and that impacted every student, every teacher, in every class, and on every day during the 1991-92 school year. Respecting the researchers caveat "not to confuse correlation with causation", this research supports the position that the Copernican change accounted for these exceptional improvements.

Please carefully observe that Chelsea's program does not reflect a shift in students due to conversion to a "magnet school" or a "choice school", where results could well be accounted for by a change in the background of the students the school serves. It does not reflect changes in the home environments and socioeconomics of students, or in the special selection of teachers. The Chelsea Trimester Program results are a consequence of an improved classroom environment.

Finally, all those who are concerned for our nation's schools, and particularly our urban schools, should tip their collective hats to the staff at Chelsea High School. Much credit belongs to a group of administrators that was willing to accept risks in their professional careers to try to salvage a year of schooling for their students, and ultimate credit goes to a large proportion of Chelsea's teachers who, even though they were not involved in a major critical decision which profoundly impacted their professional workplace, even though they had spent a summer not knowing if they had a job in September, even though they watched over a third of their colleagues lose their jobs, and even though they had never received the credit for good education which usually is reserved for the better suburban schools, rose to the occasion and used that structural opportunity to significantly improve education for their students. This has occurred when many teachers, understandably, still resent the process and still retain fears that the program presents job security risks. Still, the faculty senate supported continuing the program into the third year.

Something important has happened in education when student conduct and academic performance improves as it did in Chelsea.

A Word from the School

Chelsea High School was fortunate to have had three particularly able and dedicated administrators when the district was confronted with a devastating loss of funding: the principal, Elsa Wasserman; the two assistant principals, Andre Ravenelle and Ron Toleos. The following is a their statement to you, the reader, concerning the Chelsea Trimester Program.

"In June of 1991, three administrators were given three days to come up with a plan to provide a quality education at Chelsea High School in the face of 40% staff cuts and came up with a trimester schedule. Conventional wisdom will tell you that good jokes, good luck experiences and good runs in baseball come in sequences of three. The Chelsea High Trimester schedule could easily be seen as having been conceived in the humor of the possibility of providing a quality education with a 40% staff reduction. It has proven to be of good luck for the school through what could be considered a triple home run: Increased attendance, increased achievement and the overall improvement of the school atmosphere.

"In June, when principal Elsa Wasserman and her two assistant principals, Andre Ravenelle and Ronald Toleos went off to a Boston University meeting room to plot the possible salvaging of what could be devastating budget cuts, they brought the attitude of a tabula rasa (clean slate). With the help of Dr. Joseph Carroll and using his book, "The Copernican Plan", as a road map, we began tinkering with the tenets of secondary education: the time, the teaching and the task. The first thing which clearly had to be addressed was how to get the maximum amount of bang from the academic buck. This could clearly be done by changing the time element of the school formula. Instead of teaching five 42 minute classes a day for a year, a total of 210 minutes per day, each teacher would now teach two 95 minute classes a day for a total of 190 minutes per day. These long classes would be taught in 60 day trimesters giving a total of 6 teaching periods a year per teacher as opposed to five. With a staff of 60 teachers, this added 60 additional classes to the schedule each year.

"This system afforded the retention of a core curriculum and the complement of desperately needed electives. Students would now take a total of nine classes a year as opposed to seven. The immediate results were dramatic. This new plan was implemented in two months. With the help of a dedicated staff, school opened without a hitch. Attendance rose in the first few months by 6% from 77% daily to 81%. Serious disciplinary cases dropped from about three to five each day to about three to five per week. Suspensions the first year declined 75%. Grade retentions declined 19%. Dropouts declined 36%. The percentage of students qualifying for honor role increased by 68%. Success breeds success. This was the fundamental philosophy of the system, and because the year basically began anew every 60 days, there was a "Fresh Start" aspect to the school which encouraged achievement and success. Class sizes were kept to about 25. This was about five less than a traditional schedule would have afforded. The new schedule also meant that one teacher would only be working with about 50 students each trimester as opposed to about 150 students in a traditional schedule. The personal relationship and interaction which this affords a population which is in need of a more focused approach was remarkable.

"This "crisis" was probably the best thing that has happened to Chelsea High School in years. From the ashes of a severe 35% staff cut rose the Phoenix of more effective staff development, improved student management and an emerging effort of curriculum revision focused on the contemporary student's needs and strengths, producing a totally new model of a high school."

Elsa Wasserman, Principal
Andre Ravenelle, Assistant Principal
Ronald Toleos, Assistant Principal

MT. EVERETT REGIONAL HIGH SCHOOL
SHEFFIELD, MASSACHUSETTS
"THE ODYSSEY 2000 AND BEYOND PROGRAM"

Daily classes per teacher:	2.5
Daily classes per student:	3
Copernican Factor:	5.5

Mount Everett Regional School is located in Western Massachusetts in the Berkshire Mountains. The school serves five rural communities with a total population of about 6200. It enrolls 600 students in grades five through 12, with about 250 of these students enrolled in the high school, grades 9 through 12. Dairy and crop farming and tourism are the basic components of the local economy. Socioeconomically, the students at Mt. Everett Regional High School are predominantly from middle/lower middle income homes.

Mount Everett applied for a Massachusetts State Department of Education Carnegie (restructuring) grant in 1988 and was one of seven schools given this award. The school established a broadly based Carnegie Planning Team to guide the restructuring efforts. A series of surveys was completed which showed the parents wanted students to be more challenged, that students were looking for learning that had more meaning for them, and teachers were seeking ways to respond to the needs identified by the parents and students. Cooperative learning, learning styles, and elements of effective instruction were studied. The concepts promoted by the Coalition of Essential Schools were reviewed and the idea of the student as worker and the teacher as facilitator was one of the major objectives of the planning group.

It soon became clear that implementing all that was learned within the traditional 45-minute period was a major problem. And the students indicated they were often overwhelmed by the traditional seven period day. In the spring of 1990, the Carnegie schools visited Masconomet High School, which was then in the first year of its Copernican pilot program. This led the planning team to study its own structure and in September 1991, Mount Everett Regional High School began implementing a Copernican schedule, shown in Exhibit 11 on the following page. Exhibit 11 shows each student enrolled in three, ninety minute classes each day. Each class ran for a semester. In two semesters, the typical student should complete six classes. Teachers taught three classes in one semester and two classes in the second semester, for a total of five per year. Thus the Copernican Factor is 5.5; 3 for the students and 2.5 for the teachers.

This is a most interesting schedule for several reasons. It was developed to accommodate the "I-Courses" recommended in the Copernican Plan[24] and piloted in a similar way at Masconomet. These courses were scheduled on alternate days and backed against physical education; I-courses are scheduled for 45 minutes. These are noncredit courses which are staffed by teachers during the semester when they

Exhibit 11
The Odyssey Program

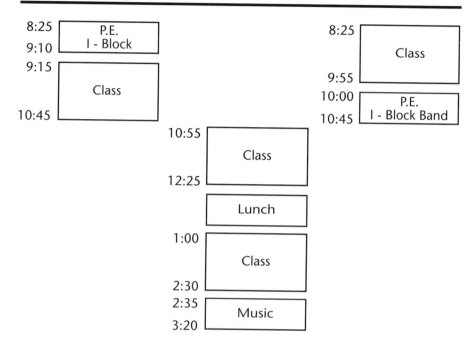

teach only two classes. A total of 27 I-Courses were offered in 1991-92, the first year under this structure; that is a large number of offerings for a small high school in its first year under a new structure.

The basic concept of the Copernican Plan is that the fundamental change in the schedule is the Copernican Change, the one that allows the other changes to be implemented successfully. Mount Everett's other changes include implementation of interdisciplinary instruction, assessment by demonstration which are strongly recommended by the Coalition of Essential Schools, and outcome based instruction which is supported in many plans and proposals including the Copernican Plan. The school is planning to implement the portfolio process "through the development of ILP's (Individualized Learning Plans)". The ILP is another concept proposed in the Copernican Plan.[25] Its utilization as part of the portfolio process is an imaginative application of the concept. What were the results obtained by Mount Everett High School in the first year under its restructured Odyssey 2000 program?

ATTENDANCE

Historically, Mount Everett has good attendance rates. In the 1990-91 school year, the high school attendance was about 95%. It was unchanged under the restructured Odyssey schedule in 1991-92.

DISCIPLINE

Mount Everett is an orderly school with relatively few serious discipline problems. Using the same Massachusetts Chapter 188 reports that were used in the case of Chelsea, the number of suspensions as a percent of enrollment was 13.1% in 1990-91, the last year under the traditional schedule, and was 14.5% in 1991-92, the first year under the Odyssey 2000 schedule. This is an increase of 11%.

DROPOUTS/RETENTION

Dropout rates have not been a major problem at Mount Everett. The dropout rate was only 3% in the 1990-91 school year and it declined to 2% in 1991-92, the first year under the Odyssey schedule. Although percentages based on small numbers tend toward the extreme, using the same analysis as used for the other schools described in this section, that is a 33% reduction in dropouts.

ACADEMIC/MASTERY

Mount Everett made impressive academic gains as a result of moving into its Odyssey 2000 schedule. Exhibit 12, found on the following page, presents an estimate of the change in academic mastery by Mount Everett students between 1990-91, the last year under the traditional schedule and 1991-92, the first year under the Odyssey program's restructured schedule. Exhibit 12 uses the same comparison of academic performance applied to the other schools in this section, which is presented in detail in previous sections. Mount Everett students improved their mastery by about 4% based on higher grades, and by about 13% based on the successful completion of more courses. Thus, the school achieved a total increase in mastery of about 17% under the Odyssey 2000 program over that achieved in the previous year under a traditional schedule, a very significant improvement in academic performance.

SUMMARY

Mount Everett's results in the first year under the Odyssey 2000's new structure are impressive and once again, fully support the Harvard team's conclusion that any high school could initiate a Copernican schedule with the expectation of academic gain. Attendance did not improve or decline.

Suspensions actually increased, which differed from the experience of other schools in this study. Dropout rates declined. Students mastered about 17% more than was the case the previous year under the traditional schedule. Very good things happened to the students at Mount Everett Regional High School as a result of this decision to restructure.

A Word From the School

Shirley Gilfeather was the assistant principal at Mt. Everett Regional High School, and she played a major role in developing the Odyssey Program. The following is her statement concerning this significant effort at restructuring.

Exhibit 12

An Estimate of Mastery of Course Content

Based Upon an Analysis of Grades Earned at Mr. Everett Regional High School,
Sheffield, Massachusetts, 1990–91 & 1991–92

Grades Earned	Traditional 1991		Copernican 1992		Diff. %	Mastery est. in %	Avg. Percent of Mastery	
	No.	%	No.	%			1991	1992
90–100 (A)	227	18%	390	28%	55%	95%	21565	37050
80–89 (B)	415	33%	502	36%	9%	85%	35275	42670
70–79 (C)	450	36%	401	28%	–20%	75%	33750	30075
60–69 (D)	96	8%	73	5%	–32%	65%	6240	4745
Below 60 (F)	79	6%	42	3%	–52%	50%	3950	2100
Total A – F	1267		1408				100780	116640
Total A – D:	1267		1408		Est. % Mastered		79.54	82.84
Enrollment	267		262		Est. Incr. in Mastery			4.1%
Courses/Student	4.75		5.37		X2 Test: P < 0.0001 (sig.)			
% Increase	—		13.2%					
Est. Total Increase in Mastery: Higher Grades and Increases in Courses Completed.*	17%							

° Assumptions upon which this estimate is based:

1. That higher grades represent a higher level of mastery. The percentages used (95% for A's, etc.) are commonly used to define these grades and represent a valid standard.
2. That the successful completion of a larger number of courses of study represents a greater mastery of course material by a student.

Sources: Mr. Everett Regional School Tabulation of Final Grades Earned by Students in 1990–91 and 1991–92.

"The ODYSSEY Program was born out of a real concern by staff, students, parents and community members that education must change to meet the needs of the 21st century. The fundamental premise was that the most important ingredient in preparing students for the future is the instruction in the classroom and that instruction encompasses *what is taught* as well as *how it is taught*. The Mt. Everett staff began retooling instructionally by participating in many staff development opportunities. Once they had developed new teaching strategies, they were frustrated by the traditional time schedule that thwarted their attempts to use the strategies. It was out of this frustration that the ODYSSEY schedule was developed. The staff continues beyond this point to seek curricular changes that build on what they have learned over the past two years about the advantages of long-block instruction.

Some of the highlights of the ODYSSEY PROGRAM from my administrative perspective are:

- concentrated focus for staff and students (3 classes per semester).
- time for strategies that emphasize student as worker, teacher as coach.
- increased preparation time for teaches to work on curricular changes.
- potential for more foreign language, and other advanced work both on and off the campus.
- involvement of students in intrinsic learning through the I-block offerings.
- revitalization of veteran staff and more frequent "fresh starts" for at risk students.

I feel professionally privileged to have been a part of the ODYSSEY program development because of its commitment to improved instruction.

Shirley Gilfeather
Assistant Principal

WEST CARTERET HIGH SCHOOL
MOREHEAD CITY, NORTH CAROLINA
"THE MACRO PROGRAM"

Daily classes per teacher:	3
Daily classes per student:	3
Copernican Factor:	6

West Carteret High School is one of two high schools in Carteret County, a coastal county in North Carolina. This school serves about 1400 students from a predominantly middle income, blue collar community. In 1989-90, West Carteret high school accounted for 80% of the county's dropouts. To solve this problem, the school applied for and received a state grant. A team was organized to develop a drop out reduction program. Since they had an assignment to reduce dropouts, not to reorganize the whole school the resulting program had to be an alternative program, a school-within-a-school, the only such program among these seven schools.

It is important to note that this team believed that "The most effective dropout deterrent is not a specialized program targeting a small sub- group but rather a more effective knowledge delivery system and an overall, pervasive change in school climate."[26] The team became aware of the Copernican Plan and after some telephone discussions, visited Masconomet during the early spring of 1991. They were serious about trying to keep students in school, and realized that the traditional approaches had not worked.

To help guide their planning, the staff had preidentified, for planning purposes only, the students most likely to drop out. In our discussions, it was emphasized that to identify the program as dropout prevention would cause many students to resist enrolling in the program and would certainly isolate those students who did enroll. Concentrating the school's potential dropouts identifies them as a group of low achievers, which could be a self-fulfilling prophesy. How could they avoid this isolation? Since the school had no tracking, it was possible to initiate a restructured program and allow any student to choose it as an option to the traditionally structured program. And the planning team felt that a very different program, such as is proposed in the Copernican Plan, would attract other students as well as students at risk.

A key factor to consider in the development of West Carteret's plans was North Carolina's testing program. All final examinations in English, math, social science, and science for all four years of high school, in every high school in the state, are state exams. Evaluation was an objective in West Carteret's planning, and evaluation of academic results, which are more difficult to obtain, could be assisted by the state's examination program. An important factor was that the North Carolina Department of Education was totally cooperative.

Keeping these factors in mind, the planning team developed a program that they called the "Macro Program", after the macroclasses proposed in the Copernican Plan. The program was neatly adapted to the West Carteret High School's situation. Exhibit 13 on the following page presents West Carteret High School's "Macro Program" schedule. Each student takes a 3hr 20 min. macroclass in the morning and each macroclass runs for a quarter of the school year, or 45 days. The students completed their English, mathematics, science, and social studies courses—the subjects for which the state provides the final examination—in these macroclasses. At the end of four quarters, the students completed four courses in the morning. In the afternoon, students could enroll in one to three electives, all taught on the traditional schedule. Thus the students could be taking three or four different classes

Exhibit 13
West Carteret High School, The Macro Program

	Typical Student Schedule			
M A C R O	English III	U.S. History	Algebra II	Chemistry
	Lunch			
P E R I O D 4	Art III			
5	French III			
6	Band			

per day, according to what each needed to graduate. Most took two traditionally scheduled courses and thus could complete six classes per year. Most importantly, students would be taking only three classes at one time as compared to the six classes they would be taking in a traditionally structured school. Please note that the traditional schedule provided for only six periods. Thus by taking three traditionally scheduled classes and one macroclass, the Macro students could complete more courses in a year than they could under a traditional program.

Teachers taught one macroclass and two traditional classes each day. Thus, each teacher taught three classes rather than five classes each day, but each teacher also taught six classes each year rather than the five classes they would teach in a traditionally scheduled year. As a result, class sizes could be 20% smaller because the teachers taught 20 % more classes each year, which is right in line with the Copernican concepts. Teachers dealt with only about fifty percent as many students each day.

West Carteret's traditional classes were 55 minutes long which provides 165 hours in a 180 day school year to complete a course of study. The 3 hour and 20 minute class (200 minutes) for 45 days (one quarter) provides 150 hours, or 9% less time.

About one hundred and fifty students enrolled in the Macro Program in the fall of 1991-92. The preidentified "at risk" students were strongly counselled to join the Macro Program and many did. As a result, 58% of the Macro students had been preidentified as "at risk" of dropping out; The remaining 42% of the students volunteered to join the Macro Program, which based on Masconomet's experience, probably indicated these students felt some dissatisfaction with the traditionally structured program. The curriculum was not changed in the macroclasses and at the end of each quarter, students took the state required final examinations in their respective courses. The first year results are most impressive.

ATTENDANCE

Attendance of this group improved from about 89% to 95%, a 6% improvement.

DISCIPLINE

The staff did not have comparative data on suspensions, but they did report that there were very few disciplinary problems with the Macro students as compared with the problems encountered in their classes in previous years or in the school as a whole. It is probable that with a group of students in which 58% had been preidentified as likely dropouts, one would expect more discipline problems.

DROPOUTS/RETENTION

The Macro Program's target was to reduce the schools dropout rate by 50%, from 11.3% to 5.6%, over a period of three years. The West Carteret High School's dropout rate fell to 4.7% in 1991-92, the first year in the Macro Program: a 58% reduction.[27] West Carteret High School met its dropout reduction target in one year.

ACADEMICS/MASTERY

The Macro Program students' grades improved remarkably. Exhibit 14, below, compares the distribution of grades during the first year of the Macro with the distribution in the previous year under a traditional schedule. Grades improved. Please note that the percentage of "A"'s increase by 119% and the percentage of "E"'s—the lowest grade that can be given—decreased by 30%. Statistically, this improved distribution of grades was significant at the .0001 level of confidence; which means that if the Macro program did not really impact the students academic performance, there would be only one chance in 10,000 of getting this difference in student performance between the two years by chance. Exhibit 14 also shows that mastery as measured in change in grades earned increased by 6.2% while mastery as measured in numbers of courses completed increased by 18.5%, a total increase of 25% in

Exhibit 14
An Estimate of Mastery of Course Content
Based Upon an Analysis of Grades Earned at West Carteret High School, Macro Program, Morehead City, North Carolina, 1990–91 & 1991–92

Grades Earned	Traditional 1991		Copernican 1992		Diff. %	Mastery est. in %	Avg. Percent of Mastery	
	No.	%	No.	%			1991	1992
A	51	6%	121	15%	124%	95%	4845	11495
B	175	22%	209	25%	13%	85%	14875	17765
C	217	28%	226	27%	–1%	75%	16275	16950
D	169	21%	169	20%	–5%	65%	10985	10985
F	175	22%	107	13%	–42%	50%	8750	5350
Total A – F	787		832				55730	62545
Total A – D	612		725		Est. % Mastered		70.81	75.17
Enrollment	140		140		Est. Incr. in Mastery			6.2%
Courses/Student	4.37		5.18		X2 Test: P < 0.0001 (sig.)			
% Increase	—		18.5%					
Est. Total Increase in Mastery: Higher Grades and Increases in Courses Completed.*	25%							

* Assumptions upon which this estimate is based:
  1. That higher grades represent a higher level of mastery. The percentages used (95% for A's, etc.) are commonly used to define these grades and represent a valid standard.
  2. That the successful completion of a larger number of courses of study represents a greater mastery of course material by a student.

  Sources: West Carteret High School tabulation of final grades earned by Macro Program Students in 1990–91 and 1991–92 school years.

mastery during the first year of the Macro Program. The Macro Program students' average scores on the North Carolina EOC (end of course) tests exceeded the state's average scores on 75% of the comparisons. Observe carefully that this record was achieved by a group of students, 58% of whom had been preidentified as at risk of dropping out.

SUMMARY

The Macro Program was immensely successful in its first year. It confirmed the planning teams' position that what was needed to reduce dropouts was a more effective knowledge delivery system and a pervasive change in school climate. In the simplest terms, students who are being talked to every day by their teachers, who feel a part of their class, and who as a result are experiencing success in school, don't drop out very often.

The success of this program, and of the Copernican Plan, is based on better relations between teachers and students and more manageable workloads for both teachers and students. The following is a partial listing of the advantages to the Macro Program as described by the West Carteret Macro staff:[28]

- Motivated students are able to graduate early.
- Sequential courses can be completed in one year. (A student could take two levels of a required subject sequentially, in one year. This was important for students trying to complete required courses for graduation.)
- Struggling at-risk students can catch-up and are often able to graduate with their class.
- Smaller classes (Each teacher teaches six classes rather than five.) and longer class time creates a more personal atmosphere.
- Class change time is converted to instructional time.
- Heterogeneous classes provide positive role models for at risk students.
- Cooperative learning activities make it possible for a teacher to emphasize shifts from competition to cooperation.
- Students who fail a Macro can often re-take that class the next quarter.
- Less motivated students are challenged to take more academic courses.
- Field trips can occur without taking students out of other classes.
- There is time to more effectively practice critical thinking skills.
- Discipline referrals decline.
- One hundred and forty additional course credits were awarded to students without additional staff or a lengthened school day. (Teachers could teach six classes per year while only teaching three classes per day.)

An impressive list of advantages, backed by solid evidence of significantly improved student performance and a major reduction in the dropout rate. The Macro program was selected as one of the leadership programs in North Carolina. A number of other high schools in North Carolina are preparing to change. In the Copernican Plan, I recommended the entire school should move to its Copernican program together, rather than deal with pilot programs. The Macro program had been identified at first as a dropout reduction effort and thus a school-within-a-school format was unavoidable. This school-within-a-school approach usually generates internal opposition, as was experienced at Masconomet. This problem has surfaced at West Carteret. However, it appears that West Carteret High School may make the school-within-a-school approach work effectively. The Macro expanded from 150 students in 1991-92 to over 400 students in the 1992-93 school year. Both two and three hour courses are being taught. The 1993-94 Macro Program will probably enroll more students, but a large increase is not expected. Teachers, primarily those teaching the AP and honors programs, are opposing its expansion; the Macro program appears to be associated with dropout prevention, and those professionals whose students appear to prosper under the traditional honors program have resisted change.

The bottom line is that something very significant has happened to the Macro students at West Carteret high school. The administrators and teachers who developed and implemented the Macro can take a great deal of pride in what they have done for their students.

A Word From The School

There was solid support from the central office and from the school for efforts to find a way to reduce West Carteret High School's drop out rate. However, there is general agreement that a very quiet, unassuming assistant principal named Beth Taylor, who also was the Macro Project Director, was the spark that ignited the program. A second key member of the team that developed this program was Anne Krouse, the Program Coordinator. Here is what they have to say about the MACRO program and the need to change high schools.

"At West Carteret High School, Macro classes (180 minute instructional blocks) have been a successful attempt to reallocate the time provided by the traditional school day into longer, more focused instructional blocks. The average high school on a six or seven period schedule expends 80 to 90 hours per year in class change time. Macro classes convert large portions of this non-productive time into instructional time by decreasing the number of classes per day and by increasing the time spent in each class. At West, both 180 minute quarter classes and 110 minute semester classes are being offered in conjunction with the traditional 55 minute linear courses. (Author's note: The 110 minute classes were introduced in the second year of the MACRO Program; the first year was used for this evaluation.)

"Macro scheduling is a positive innovation for students, teachers, administrators and parents. Parent comments have been overwhelmingly positive and supportive, primarily because students are taking and passing more courses, are making better grades, are generally out-performing non-macro students on state mandated end-of-course tests and are sharing with parents positive comments about specific courses and their involvement in school. Macro periods provide a framework within which a teacher has time to introduce a concept as well as discuss, internalize and apply that concept, involve students in group work, provide guided practice activities, review, test for mastery and re-teach if necessary, all within one instructional period.

"Macro teachers have more time to plan for effective instruction because they teach a reduced number of subjects, sections and students on a daily basis. In the traditional system, teachers generally teach 5 classes of 30 students per day with one planning period. Macro teachers teach more than 5 classes across the span of a year but fewer classes and fewer students on a daily basis. Large instructional blocks also enhance the use of cooperative learning group activities.

Students enrolled in smaller macro classes enjoy a more positive teacher/student relationship which enhances all aspects of the learning process. The longer instructional period and use of cooperative learning techniques provide an atmosphere which fosters affirming relationships between students and between students and teachers. Macro students profit from a more focused learning environment that provides time for integration of material and effective group interaction. They have fewer subjects to manage on a daily bias, yet they take more subjects and earn more credits each year. Marginal students can catch up and more motivated students can accelerate and either take more courses than are required or graduate early in order to pursue post secondary educational or employment opportunities. Students can take several sequential courses in one year (i.e. French I and French II or Algebra I, Geometry, Algebra II) and retake failed courses immediately. Students who find it necessary to drop out of school can return during the school year and still earn credits toward graduation. The six or seven period linear school year cannot provide returning students with this kind of service. The macro classes allow seniors needing only one credit to graduate the opportunity to complete that credit by November whereas the traditional system demands a full year commitment and usually requires the student to carry four or five additional courses that are not required for graduation. This student takes up much needed space and is frequently an attendance or discipline problem. Block scheduling offers a dejuvenilized environment that provides more opportunities for students to make decisions about their educational program.

"Administrators review effective schools data and dream of a school with a strong attendance profile, high overall grade point average, solid test scores, reduced discipline referrals and positive student attitudes toward school and learning. Large block instruction delivers on all counts. Given a choice, larger instructional blocks with few classes per day (180 minutes twice per day) wins hands down. Scheduling is simplified, non-instructional class change time is minimized, students and teachers have only two preps daily (often only one for teachers), tests and papers must be graded for only 30 to 40 students rather than 150 students, make-up is simplified, new students and drop-outs can enroll four times during the year and seriously ill students or students with chronic attendance problems can dropout for one quarter and still accumulate 6 credits for the year.

"The American school system is a modern-day Titanic. It is sinking in deep waters while many educators appear to be unaware. The overwhelming problems of education cannot be solved by rearranging deck chairs...an extensive overhaul is required. Now is not the time for timid reform efforts. School must change. Students can't afford to wait for the system to be entirely "broken" before it is fixed and the "wheel" must be repaired before it squeaks. Reformers can not fall prey to nay-sayers who present all the problems a new approach might create. There exists within every school system among teachers, students, support staff, administrators, parents and community a veritable gold mine of positive creative problem solving ability to take a proven new approach and make it work effectively for all students.

> Beth Taylor, Project Director
> Anne Krouse, Project Coordinator

LONGMONT HIGH SCHOOL
LONGMONT, COLORADO
FOUR BLOCK SCHEDULE

Daily classes per teacher: 3
Daily classes per student: 4
Copernican Factor: 7

Longmont High School is one of three high schools serving Longmont, Colorado, a small city about 40 miles north of Denver. Longmont enrolls about 1200 students, grades 9 through 12. The school serves an attendance area that is described as middle to upper middle, socioeconomically; about 11% of Longmont's students are minorities, mostly Hispanic. The school operated under a traditional seven period day with students enrolling in six courses and teachers teaching five classes each day. Periods were 50 minutes in length. The school has a good reputation as an effective high school in an attractive community. The Longmont staff, while not pressured by problems to change, simply felt that they could do better by their students.

After examining the research and the experience of some other high schools having nontraditional schedules, the school decided in 1991-92 to restructure, and chose to implement a Four Block Schedule. Exhibit 15, which is found on the following page, presents the Four Block Schedule. Students would enroll in four, 90 minute macroclasses each day. Juniors and seniors had the option to enroll in only three courses to accommodate jobs or to reduce pressures during an athletic season or some other activity. Each macroclass would run for 90 days or a semester. The traditional classes were 50 minutes in length and ran for 180 days, which provided 150

Exhibit 15
Longmont High School Block Schedule

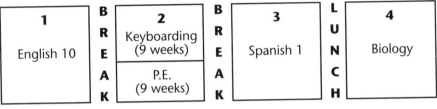

Typical Student Schedule

First Semester

1	B R E A K	2	B R E A K	3	L U N C H	4
English 10		Keyboarding (9 weeks) / P.E. (9 weeks)		Spanish 1		Biology

Second Semester

1	B R E A K	2	B R E A K	3	L U N C H	4
World History		Geometry		P.E. (9 weeks) / Crafts (9 weeks)		An Extra Elective Block

Under the block schedule, full year courses are completed in 18 weeks or in one semester. Traditional semester courses are completed in nine weeks or one quarter of the year. Students complete courses in less time than under the traditional schedule, thus allowing students to complete eight courses per year.

hours to complete a course; The Four Block schedule provided 135 hours, or 9% less total time. Teachers would teach three macroclasses each day, or six each year, thus gaining the advantage of an approximately 20% reduction in class size which is available under this format. Let us review the results of the first year in this Four Block structure.

ATTENDANCE

Attendance at Longmont High School has traditionally been very good and in 1990-91, the last year under the traditional schedule, the school had a 96.3% rate of attendance. In 1991-92, the first year under the Four Block Schedule, attendance was 94.2% which is good. Applying the same evaluative process as used in the other schools, it is a decline of 2.2%.

SUSPENSIONS

Longmont was unable to provide suspension data in the format required for this evaluation; Colorado does not require this information to be reported.

DROPOUTS

Longmont High School's dropout rates have been traditionally very low. In 1990-91, its dropout rate was only 1.6%. In 1991-92, the dropout rate was 2.6% which is still a low rate. Following the pattern of evaluation applied to the other schools in this study, it is, proportionally, an increase of 63%. The size of this increase reflects the small numbers involved. This is the only increase in dropout rate reported by these seven schools.

ACADEMICS/MASTERY

Longmont High School achieved substantial gains in mastery during its first year under the Four Block Schedule. Exhibit 16, which is presented on the following page, shows the percentage of A's increased by 20% and the percentage of F's decreased by 30% during the first year under the Copernican structure. As a result, mastery as represented by higher grades increased by 2.5%. Since the students had an opportunity to enroll in eight courses during a year, mastery as measured by courses completed increased by 15.5%. The total increase in mastery was about 18%, an impressive improvement.

SUMMARY

Longmont's decision to move to the Four Block Schedule has been fully justified by these results. The students have learned more in their courses and have completed more courses. The declines in percentage of attendance and the increase in the percentage of dropouts probably reflects the impact on students of dealing with four macroclasses at one time. It is an impressive first year and fully supports the Harvard Team's prediction that introducing a Copernican schedule will result in pedagogical gains for students.

A Word From The School

H. D. ("Duke") Aschenbrenner, principal of Longmont High School, has provided effective leadership in introducing the Four Block Schedule. Here are his thoughts concerning change at Longmont and change in general.

"I have been a secondary principal for nineteen years, and I have been at Longmont High School for fourteen years. In all those years, I have never experienced the excitement, the stress, or the satisfaction that has come from restructuring our school schedule and our instructional mission.

The LHS staff pursued restructuring with two priorities in mind. We wanted to make the day more humane and conducive to education, and we wanted to make the students more active in and more responsible for their own learning. The schedule we chose was a four block or period, ninety minute day with extended breaks between classes and a common lunch period. This school schedule has many advantages. It focuses student's attention on fewer courses at any given time, and it

Exhibit 16
An Estimate of Mastery of Course Content
Based Upon an Analysis of Grades Earned at Longmont High School, Longmont, Colorado, 1990–91 & 1991–92

Grades Earned	Traditional 1991 No.	%	Copernican 1992 No.	%	Diff. %	Mastery est. in %	Avg. Percent of Mastery 1991	1992
A	3571	31%	6898	38%	20%	95%	339245	655310
B	3186	28%	5152	28%	0%	85%	270810	437920
C	2307	20%	3179	17%	−14%	75%	173025	238425
D	1311	12%	1937	11%	−8%	65%	85215	125905
F	965	9%	1090	6%	−33%	50%	48250	54500
Total A – F	11340		18256				916545	1512060
Total A –D:	10375		17166		Est. % Mastered		80.82	82.83
Enrollment	836		1198		Est. Incr. in Mastery			2.5%
Courses/Student	12.41		14.33		X2 Test: P < 0.0001 (sig.)			
% Increase	—		15.5%					
Est. Total Increase in Mastery: Higher Grades and Increases in Courses Completed.*	18%							

°Assumptions upon which this estimate is based:
  1. That higher grades represent a higher level of mastery. The percentages used (95% for A's, etc.) are commonly used to define these grades and represent a valid standard.
  2. That the successful completion of a larger number of courses of study represents a greater mastery of course material by a student.
  Sources: Longmont High School records regarding distribution of grades and enrollments for 1990–91 and 1991–92.

concentrates the students learning. At the same time, the block schedule has effectively personalized education because teachers have only three classes of students at one time and the students only three or four teachers in any given term. The block schedule humanizes the school routine or day. While increasing the concentration on education, it decreases the stress and harried feeling of a typical day in a traditional American high school.

However, while the most outwardly noticeable, the block schedule is not the actual restructuring or reform at LHS. The block schedule is the tool we used to implement our instructional mission. The instructional changes are the true reforms we have successfully made. A ninety minute class period requires the teacher to change instructional approaches. Within any class period, several activities and teaching strategies must be used to keep students engaged in learning. It was amazingly rewarding to actually watch this instructional revolution take place in the classrooms of the school. I saw teachers grow and stretch and embrace the challenge of the school's new instructional goals. Morale rose higher and higher as success became more evident. I can safely say that the quality of education has never been better at LHS.

I encourage other educational leaders to accept the challenge of improving the American high school. To any who would pursue such change, I would make the following suggestions.

1. If a school is going to restructure, its staff must develop a philosophy which reflects the priorities it has identified. In a time of change and reform, it is easy for a staff to "shop" for novel ideas. However, for restructuring to be truly successful, a staff must know why changes are being made; it must have a shared vision.

2. It is my belief that a principal or an administrative team alone does not restructure a high school. True change requires the teaching staff "own" the change and share the vision and the goals driving the restructuring efforts. Longmont High School's restructuring movement was designed by the staff and implemented by the staff. As the principal, I supported their efforts and championed their cause.

3. The school's leaders must be the "keeper of the vision". The principal facilitates the change. From hiring staff members who are aligned with the school's vision, to supporting teachers in making the transition to new instructional expectations, the school's leadership must protect and polish the school's mission.

The experience I have had with the change process has been one of the most challenging, but most satisfying periods of my career. Some say the American high school cannot be significantly changed because of the outside forces which affect it. However, the LHS staff has found the opposite to be true over the last three years. LHS is an improved high school which is dynamic, innovative and attuned to the needs of today's students. I encourage other schools and school leaders to consider reforms. Change is not easy, but in our case at least, it has certainly been worth the extra work and risk."

Sincerely,
H.D. Aschenbrenner
Principal

Daily classes per teacher: 3
Daily classes per student: 4
Copernican Factor: 7

Rocky Mountain High School serves about 1200 students coming from a middle income community in Fort Collins, Colorado. It is one of three high schools serving Fort Collins, and the three schools are described as fairly similar, socioeconomically. Rocky Mountain High School's staff became aware of the substantial criticism of the American high school and of the research that supported that criticism. In 1988-89, Rocky Mountain staff initiated a restructuring process that began with a mission statement and involved a great deal of analysis of the research and various options for restructuring. The staff visited a number of restructured schools including the May 1990 conference at Masconomet and several visits to Wasson High School in Colorado Springs.

In September, 1992, Rocky Mountain initiated the Rocky Mountain Model following the four block schedule which was initiated by Wasson High School in September 1990 and which was implemented by Longmont High School in September 1991. The Copernican factor and the format was the same. The total process was very well planned, was not rushed, and included staff development in the areas of teaching strategies for the 90-minute block and effective instructional techniques. About 80% of the Rocky Mountain teachers favored moving the school to this Copernican model.

Rocky Mountain High School's restructuring appeared to the staff to be very successful and near the end of the first year, 85% of the teachers voted to continue the program, an increase over the percentage of teachers supporting the program as it began. However, as the year progressed, opposition to this restructuring plan developed, led by about 20 parents and with some support by school board members. The group's criticism, which surfaced quite often in the local press, seemed to center on the students not being able to learn as much. One of the key complaints was that the 90 minute period for a semester provided 18% less total time to complete a course than was provided under the 55 minute period for 180 days.

In July of 1993, Dr. Karen Dixon, the principal, called me because she was concerned that the program might be terminated by this criticism. She was particularly concerned about the reaction of her teachers if they returned and found a change that they felt had been so productive and that they had strongly supported, had been terminated. Certainly, this was an emotion I could share.

I asked for the data used in this evaluation and Dr. Dixon expedited its delivery. Thus I was able to include Rocky Mountain High School in this evaluation. Let us consider what happened to students at this high school as a result of the staff's decision to go Copernican.

ATTENDANCE

Attendance was a satisfactory 92.72% in 1991-92, the last year under a traditional schedule. It was 93.61% in 1992-93 under the Copernican structure, a 1% increase.

SUSPENSIONS

Rocky Mountain is an orderly school with very few suspensions. However, suspensions did drop from 16 in 1991-92 to only 10 in 1992-93. This is a 38% decline in suspensions, applying the same evaluative format used with the other schools to these data. However, percentages tend to magnify changes when dealing with small numbers. Nonetheless, suspensions decreased in a year when the enrollment increased 6%. This is a substantial improvement and correlates well with the suspension reductions presented for the other schools presented above.

DROPOUTS

The dropout rate at Rocky Mountain High school in 1991-92 was 4%. This rate dropped to 2.3% in 1992-93, a reduction of 42.5%, during the first year under the Copernican schedule. Again, we are dealing with small numbers which generate large percentages. However, this significant decline in dropouts parallels the reduction in dropout rates in the other schools presented above.

ACADEMICS/MASTERY

Exhibit 17, which is shown on the following page, presents a comparison of mastery of course content based on an analysis of grades earned by Rocky Mountain High School students in 1991-92 with the grades earned in 1992-93 under a Copernican structure. Exhibit 17 finds that mastery as a result of higher grades increased 1.4%. Mastery as measured in courses successfully completed increased by 20.0%, a very solid increase reflecting the fact that the students had an opportunity to complete eight classes per year under the Copernican structure as compared with six per year under the traditional structure. In total, mastery improved by 21.4%, a very significant improvement.

SUMMARY

The decision by the Rocky Mountain staff to restructure and to initiate a Copernican schedule has, once again, solidly supported the Harvard Evaluation Team's conclusion that a high school can initiate a Copernican schedule with an expectation of pedagogical gain. A great deal that is good has happened to these 1200 students. And it is still happening; the program continues. The evaluative data appeared to be useful in supporting the program's continuation.

Exhibit 17
An Estimate of Mastery of Course Content
Based Upon an Analysis of Grades Earned at Rocky Mountain High School, Fort Collins, Colorado, 1990–91 & 1991–92

Grades Earned	Traditional 1991 No.	%	Copernican 1992 No.	%	Diff. %	Mastery est. in %	Avg. Percent of Mastery 1991	1992
A	5841	43%	7858	46%	7%	95%	554895	746510
B	3513	26%	4588	27%	4%	85%	298605	389980
C	2227	16%	2587	15%	−7%	75%	167025	194025
D	1176	9%	1511	7%	−22%	65%	76440	74815
F	764	6%	784	5%	−18%	50%	38200	39200

Total A – F	13521	16184		1135165 1444530
Total A – D:	12757	16184	Est. % Mastered	83.96 85.13
Enrollment	1213	1282	Est. Incr. in Mastery	1.4%
Courses/Student	10.52	12.62	X2 Test: P < 0.0001 (sig.)	
% Increase	—	20.0		

Est. Total Increase in Mastery: Higher Grades and Increases in Courses Completed.*	21%

°Assumptions upon which this estimate is based:
1. That higher grades represent a higher level of mastery. The percentages used (95% for A's, etc.) are commonly used to define these grades and represent a valid standard.
2. That the successful completion of a larger number of courses of study represents a greater mastery of course material by a student.

Sources: Rocky Mountain High School records regarding distribution of grades and enrollments for 1990–91 and 1991–92.

A Word from the School

The administrators that led these Copernican changes are strong people, but each is strong in different ways. Karen Dixon's strengths certainly include dedication, perseverance, and candor, as will be shown in the following statement.

"I have been a high school principal for the past three and one half years. During that time, I have focused on school reform. The Rocky Mountain High School staff responded favorably to focusing on the issues of raising academic achievement for all students, providing a more humane environment for students and staff, looking at the way we used time, and focusing on the importance of the relationships between students and teachers in the learning process.

The first two years centered on developing a mission statement and adopting a set of beliefs about teaching and learning. Later all ideas were evaluated on the basis of whether they supported and advanced our mission and beliefs.

During our restructuring process, the Poudre R-1 School District had four different superintendents who had different views on educational reform. As the principal, I was supervised by three different executives. Also, the teacher association president has changed twice. Therefore, my primary support and direction came from my leadership team, my staff, my community and my desire to make a difference.

Other initiatives were going on simultaneously that demanded time, effort, and commitment by staff. Rocky Mountain was involved in a fifteen million dollar construction project. In addition, Rocky Mountain was reviewed by our regional accrediting association. Our self study focused on the areas of communication, teaching strategies, and diversity which supported our restructuring efforts.

As I reflect on the past five years, there are a number of, what I believe to be, important insights I gained during our restructuring process. During the first four years of research, planning, and development of our alternative delivery system, we involved all of our constituencies including parents, staff, students, and other community members. Parents were involved through two series of coffees, students through student council and small group interaction with administrators, staff through meetings and inservice, and community through special meetings. However, since we graduate a class after three years, by the time we implemented our system, many of our students, parents and staff were no longer a part of our Rocky Mountain community. One suggestion I have is to form a marketing committee in your school that focuses on public relations and communication. Communication must include information about the evaluation of your changes. On-going evaluation with predetermined criteria is essential.

The staff need continual opportunities for growth, time to rethink their teaching strategies, and encouragement and support in an environment where they can risk and feel safe. During the four years of planning and the first year of implementation, we had an extensive staff development program in place. The focus of the staff development was on cooperative learning, learning styles, thinking skills, and strategies for the 90 minute block. Many staff members participated beyond the required inservice time, others chose not to participate. Seminars were offered which allowed staff opportunities to talk with their colleagues about teaching and learning and to share successes and failures. Seminars provided time for staff to form a network of support for each other.

During the first year of implementation, staff needed continued encouragement, support, and attention. Comments were made such as " I feel like a beginning teachers again" or "I am exhausted" by teachers who had 20 years of experience. How easily confidence can be shaken. Teachers who reported that they tried to teach two 55-minute lessons in one 90 minute period were frustrated. It didn't work. Those who looked at 90 minutes of instruction were more successful and less stressed.

What I learned as a leader was that change does not happen as quickly as I would like; patience is an important characteristic. You cannot "beam" a whole group of people forward at one time. Change is very personal and leaders have to work with each individual.

Leaders must be grounded in their philosophy of teaching and learning and stay committed to their mission and beliefs. If you know where you are headed, it will be easier to take the criticism that comes with change. There will be pressure to return to the status quo. When that doesn't happen, individuals personally attack the leader's skills, professional judgment, and character. A leader must have stamina, persistence and confidence. What kept me going was knowing that I was doing the right thing for students.

Another critical skill a leader must have is the capacity to deal with sabotage. The sabotage will come from within the organization and from those outside the organization. How a leader deals with sabotage will define whether you move forward or regress backward. Pressure will come to solve the conflict and return to the status quo. I had to learn to live with the conflict and the pressure. During these times, your staff needs and expects you to take a stand and support them.

In summary, change is difficult. Boards of education, business, parents, staff, and students speak of needed changes in the educational system, but when you change, there will be pressure to return to the status quo by even those who demand change. I encourage leaders to take a strong stand on what you believe in, be persistent, stay the course, have a strong support system, and believe in yourself and your staff. Our motto at Rocky Mountain High School is " Knowledge is our future". I will take that one step farther. Kids are our future, and we owe it to them to move ahead despite all the obstacles and pressures to do nothing. The data we have gathered shows an increase in academic achievement, a decrease in the dropout rate, and an increase in the attendance rate. I believe in my staff and will continue to support them as we continue to evaluate and move forward.

Karen Dixon, Principal
Rocky Mountain High School

GREEN RIVER HIGH SCHOOL
GREEN RIVER, WYOMING
"ROTATING BLOCK SCHEDULE"

Classes at one time per teacher:	6
Classes at one time per student:	8
Copernican Factor:	14
Daily classes per teacher:	4
Daily classes per student:	3
Copernican Factor:	7

Green River High School serves approximately 1050 students who reside in the ranching and mining community centered in Green River, a small city in western Wyoming. Green River is recognized as one of Wyoming's good high schools. It has a supportive community, modern facilities, and it takes pride in the staff development it provides for its staff, and with good reason. The district's staff development program has high priority and support from the school board, is well planned on a multiyear basis, and addresses the following areas of professional development: TESA (Teacher Expectations and Student Achievement), Qualities of Instruction (based on Madeline Hunter's work), a Clinical Supervision program, Cooperative Learning training (a key element for teaching most effectively in macroclasses), Learning Styles, Assertive Discipline, and Tactics for Thinking. Every year some Green River teachers are provided tuition and room costs to attend summer programs at Seattle Pacific University. As part of this professional development program, a team from Green River visited Masconomet's Renaissance Program in the spring of 1990 and as a follow up, brought Masconomet staff to Green River to share their experiences with the Green River High School staff, who were considering possible implementation of the Copernican Plan.

The planning for this change was also well done. It was a careful process which was completed during the 1990-91 school year. The decision to move to a new structure, the Rotating Block Schedule, had solid support and the entire school moved at one time. Based on surveys taken at the end of September 1991, the first month under the Copernican Schedule, about 90% of the parents and 85% of the students gave positive responses[29], so the program got off to a good start.

The Rotating Block Schedule is presented in Exhibit 18, found on the following page. The traditional schedule that preceded it provided a seven period day for students and teachers taught six periods, or a Copernican Factor of 13. The Rotating Block Schedule placed students in three 91 minute classes (periods 2, 3,and 5) on "A" day and three other 91 minute classes (periods 1, 4,and 6) on "B" day; the schedule shifted from A to B and back again every other day for the full school year. Period 7 was a 60 minute class which met Monday through Thursday throughout the year. Period 7 on Fridays was used for special programs, which was conceptually somewhat like the seminars recommended in the Copernican Plan. Thus the students continued to take seven classes at one time but only four per day and teachers continued to teach six classes at one time, but only three each day. A question arises: What is the Copernican Factor for the Rotating Block Schedule?

On a daily basis, the Copernican Factor drops from 13 under the traditional schedule to 7 under the Rotating Block Schedule. But is the net impact on teacher workload factors in terms of numbers of students and the range of curricula which must be dealt with concurrently really very different? Similarly, are student workloads in terms of the numbers of courses which students must manage and the number of teachers with whom students must relate concurrently really very different? If not, then the Copernican factor increases to 14. The answer to this question may be reflected in the evaluation data.

The Green River structure emphasizes the longer class, the macroclass, as the single major change. Theoretically, this change should be reflected in improved student teacher relations. It sharply reduces the probability of a heavy over night homework assignment and allows students and teachers to deal with fewer classes each day. It is, conceptually, quite different from the restructuring of the other schools presented above, since all courses run for the full year.

Exhibit 18
Green River High School Rotating Block Schedule

Day	A M	B T	A W	B TH	A F	B M	A T	B W	A TH	B F
P 7:45 9:16	2	1	2	1	2	1	2	1	2	1
E 9:22 9:37	**Channel One**					**Channel One**				
R 9:37 11:08	3	4	3	4	3	4	3	4	3	4
11:08 11:48	**Lunch**					**Lunch**				
I 11:53 1:24	5	6	5	6	5	6	5	6	5	6
O 1:30 2:30	7	7	7	7	TBA	7	7	7	7	TBA
D 2:30 2:45	**Tutorials Makeups**					**Tutorials Makeups**				

Let us review the results as we did in the previous cases, by comparing various student performance measures in the 1990-91 school year, the year before Green River High School implemented its Copernican Schedule with those for 1991-92, the first year under its new schedule.

ATTENDANCE

Attendance at Green River High School in the 1990-91 school year was 97%, an excellent record.[30] In 1991-92 under the Copernican schedule, attendance dropped to 92.3%, which is a 9% drop but is still good attendance. Nonetheless, it is one of two schools reporting a drop in attendance.

SUSPENSIONS

Exhibit 19 on page 63 shows that suspensions declined 57% during the first year under this version of a Copernican structure. That is a very significant improvement and it supports the results achieved at other schools, particularly at Chelsea.

The Copernican Plan Evaluated

Exhibit 19

A Comparision of the Rates of Suspension at Green River High School, Green River, Wyoming, 1990–91 and 1991–92

	1990–91 Traditional	1991–92 Copernican
Enrollment Grades 9–12	1055	1073
Suspensions:		
In-School	44	6
Out of School	294	148
Total	338	154
Suspensions As a Percent of Enrollment	32.0%	13.8%
Suspensions declined about 57% during the first year of the rotating block schedule		

Sources: Green River High School Registrar's Records
for 1990–91 and 1991–92.

DROPOUTS

In 1990-91, Green River High School's dropout rate was 6%; in 1991-92, under the new structure it fell to 5%, which is a 17% reduction. That is a significant improvement when viewed in context. As was noted in considering Chelsea, Massachusetts' dropout prevention grants achieved only an 11% improvement in a three year period.[31]

ACADEMICS/MASTERY

From an evaluation/research perspective, the most interesting information concerning Green River High School's new structure is its impact on academics. Exhibit 20, on the following page, presents an estimate of mastery of course content based upon an analysis of grades earned by students at Green River High School in 1990-91 and 1991-92; the same comparison shown for all the high schools previously reviewed. Grades declined in 1991-92, the first year under the Copernican schedule, as compared to 1990-91 under the traditional program. The largest change was in the increase in the failure rate from 2% to 5%. The net decline in the estimate of mastery was a -0.5%. The students enrolled in more courses and successfully completed more courses under the Rotating Block Schedule which accounted for a .2% increase in mastery. The net result was no difference in mastery between these two years.

Exhibit 20

An Estimate of Mastery of Course Content

Based Upon an Analysis of Grades Earned at Green River High School, Green River, Wyoming, 1990–91 & 1991–92

Grades Earned	Traditional 1991 No.	Traditional 1991 %	Copernican 1992 No.	Copernican 1992 %	Diff. %	Mastery est. in %	Avg. Percent of Mastery 1991	Avg. Percent of Mastery 1992
A	4231	35%	4704	37%	6%	95%	401945	446880
B	3751	31%	3553	28%	–10%	85%	318835	302005
C	2336	19%	2438	19%	0%	75%	175200	182850
D	1302	11%	1200	9%	–12%	65%	84630	78000
Pass	253	2%	210	2%	0%	70%	17710	14700
F	222	2%	580	5%	149%	50%	11100	29000

Total A – F:	12095	12685		1009420	1053435
Total A – Pass:	11873	12105	Est. % Mastered	83.46	83.05
Enrollment	1055	1073	Est. Incr. in Mastery		–0.5%
Courses/Student	11.25	11.28	X2 Test: P < 0.0001 (sig.)		
% Increase	—	0.2%			

Est. Total Increase in Mastery: Higher Grades and Increases in Courses Completed.*	0%

*Assumptions upon which this estimate is based:

1. That higher grades represent a higher level of mastery. The percentages used (95% for A's, etc.) are commonly used to define these grades and represent a valid standard.

2. That the successful completion of a larger number of courses of study represents a greater mastery of course material by a student.

Sources: Green River High School registrar's records regarding for 1990–91 and 1991–92.

SUMMARY

Clearly, Green River High School's decision to move to a Copernican structure has resulted in some substantial gains in terms of student teacher relationships as reflected in the measures of suspensions and dropouts. However, attendance did decline. The net impact, academically, tells a very different story. This is the only Copernican model that did not show an increase in mastery, and all the other increases were double digit. The impact measured by grades found the only decline among these seven schools, albeit a small one. Students made only a slight gain in the number of courses completed successfully. These academic results differ sharply from those obtained under the other Copernican models. Later, I will consider the significance of these results in the context of the results from all the schools.

A Word from the School

Craig Butler is the warm, friendly, and effective principal of Green River High School. He is a fine educator, and he takes considerable pride in his school and his staff. Here is his message to you concerning the Green River restructuring process.

"It is certainly a privilege to include this letter in Dr. Carroll's new book as a reflection of our efforts to restructure Green River High School. I believe the school improvement process is on going and you basically never arrive, but rather just continue to improve the quality of education.

At Green River High School our decision in 1990 to restructure was based on the belief of the teachers and administrators that doing what we were doing was not achieving what we wanted. The arrangement of fifty or fifty-five minute class periods, while experiencing several passing periods, was not the best way of maximizing instructional time each day. Over eighty per cent of our teachers were supportive of our desire to drastically lengthen class periods and greatly reduce the number of passing periods each day. In addition, as a result of the longer class periods, we were trying to create an opportunity where cooperative learning, creative teaching, extra guided practice, mastery learning, and relationship building would be the norm. While, some teachers just doubled what they were doing before, many restructured their efforts to enact new freedom in exploring varied teaching techniques and engaging students in useful learning.

Although we are still changing and modifying our structure, our ultimate goal is to set up an environment for teachers to do their best teaching, and students to learn according to their learning style. Longer class periods hopefully have allowed our teachers to deliver useful information in a multitude of meaningful ways. I contend that our previous shorter periods did not allow for such flexibility. I think a big indicator is that our surveys have shown that nearly 90% of the students prefer the longer classes on the alternating basis. Students mention many benefits, the least of which is that it is "less stressful".

I hope our experience will be helpful to you in your restructuring efforts. I look forward to sharing information with each of you in the future as well.

Sincerely,
Craig B. Butler, Principal
Green River High School"

OTHER HIGH SCHOOLS

Other high schools have switched to Copernican schedules but only those schools with one or more years of experience and which could provide the appropriate baseline data could be considered for inclusion in this study. Few schools are in their second or third year under a Copernican structure. However, comments from some of these other schools provides useful information.

Caledonia High School in Caledonia, Michigan, a suburb of Grand Rapids, implemented a trimester Copernican program in September 1990 and the program is now in its third year. The principal, Tonya Porter, was very cooperative in discussing Caledonia's program. She believes the program has been very successful and particularly in developing good relations between teachers and students. Assessments of program effectiveness were developed internally. This program included a "Challenge Time", which was similar to the seminars recommended in the Copernican Plan and included in Masconomet's program. Also paralleling Masconomet's experience, this part of the program had mixed success, which reinforces the need for more careful planning for seminars. Caledonia is encountering some pressure because of less total time to complete a course under the trimester format. The opposition seems to be coming primarily from parents of students enrolled in honors classes. This also parallels the experience at Masconomet, and other schools have given similar reports. Caledonia High School has been very available to help other high schools considering restructuring, and a number of Michigan high schools are reported to be considering Copernican models.

Independence High School in Columbus, Ohio initiated a Copernican program called "Project Tri", which is very similar to the Chelsea Trimester in terms of the structure. Independence High School is an urban high school which enrolls about 900 students and which deals with most of the problems of our nation's urban schools. The school is in its first year in 1992-93 and thus does not have the data needed for inclusion in this evaluation. However, its midyear reports are remarkably similar to those of Chelsea High School during its first year. For example, attendance improved from 87% in 1991-92 to 95% for the first semester of 1992-93; from sixth to first place among Columbus' seventeen high schools. An interim report on suspensions indicates a 15% decline over the previous year. The numbers of students on the honor rolls has doubled.[32] The program is part of the Coalition of Essential Schools and has developed a partnership with Ohio State University's School of Education. Independence High School has had a substantial number of visitations and has been very generous in helping neighboring high schools in their restructuring plans.

Rutland Senior Secondary School: Eight secondary schools in British Columbia are implementing the L.V.Rogers High School's Horizontal Timetable, with variations to accommodate local conditions and objectives. However, all are in their first year. All are reporting success similar to that achieved by L.V.Rogers in its pioneering first year. The number of schools utilizing the Horizontal Timetable is likely to increase in 1993-94.

The experience of one of these schools is most unusual, and points to the value of being able to "start school" four times each year instead of only once in September.[33] Rutland Senior Secondary School was considered to be somewhat less prestigious than the other secondary schools which served Kolowna, British Columbia. In 1991-92, the school enrolled 660 students. Many local students opted to attend other high schools. It adopted the Horizontal Timetable in September 1992. Its September enrollment was 972, 47% more than enrolled the previous year and over 20% greater than its projections, which anticipated a return of dropouts, most of whom had been prevented from graduating by failure in the provincial 12th grade exams. At the end of the first quarter, 30 students were able to graduate, as compared to only 4 students who graduated in midyear during the previous year under a traditional schedule. However, the second quarter's enrollment was still 971 students, as more former students returned to school to complete their secondary educations. Another 34 students completed graduation requirements at the end of the second quarter. Attendance has increased from 85% in 1991-92 to 93% for the first two quarters. Similarly, the percentage of students passing all courses jumped from 84% in the previous year to 94% for the first two quarters. The percentage of A or B grades jumped from 39% the previous year to 49% for the first two quarters of the 1991-93 school year. Ninety eight percent of the students passed their 12th grade provincial exams and approximately a quarter of the exam grades are at the level to qualify for the provincial scholarships. The principal and staff are excited about their students' success. One teacher commented, tongue-in- cheek, that because of overcrowding, they "can't afford to be much more successful"! What a wonderful dilemma.

Omak High School serves about 500 students from a rural community near the eastern slopes of the Cascade mountains in Washington. Approximately a quarter of the school's students are minorities, primarily Native Americans. In the spring of 1990, a team from Omak visited Masconomet as part of its planning for restructuring. After a year of planning, a Four Block Schedule, similar to the schedules reported above for Longmont and Rocky Mountain high schools, was initiated. It should be noted that 87% of the Omak teachers voted to make this change.[34] Omak was recognized by the Washington State Department of Education for its excellent planning process.

Omak planned an evaluation as part of its overall restructuring plan, and Dick Neimeyer, the school's principal, shared all of this information with the author. Unfortunately, the baseline academic data needed to be included as one of the schools in this evaluation was not available due to limitations in the computer system. Attendance and dropout data reported to the state was unchanged. However, data on suspensions showed a 33% reduction in the first year under a Copernican Schedule as compared with the previous year's under the traditional schedule.

Part III

Copernican Messages from this Experience

The experience of all seven high schools included in this study, strongly supports the conclusion of the Harvard Evaluation that "Implementing a Copernican style schedule can be accomplished with the expectation of favorable pedagogical outcomes." These are very different schools, using very different Copernican schedules. These schools experienced significant improvements, improvements of orders of magnitude seldom if ever reported from a group of our nation's high schools.[35]

But let us analyze this experience in more depth in order to answer questions which these evaluations may raise and to identify the messages that this information provides those responsible for the planning, organization, and administration of our nation's high schools.

1. Are these schools representative?

These eight schools, in total, are a fairly representative cross section of our nation's high schools. Masconomet is known as a high performing suburban high school, with a strong reputation as a fine school. L.V. Rogers is a very good high school which reflects Canadian experience, experience that can be easily applied to schools in the United States. Green River reflects the culture and experience of high schools serving small, nonsuburban cities. West Carteret High School serves part of a typical southern county school system and draws a majority of its enrollments from lower middle income neighborhoods, which is reflected in its concern about its drop out rate. Chelsea High School is a prototype of a difficult urban school and its problems and experience would be applicable to most urban schools. Longmont High School serves an upper income neighborhood in a major metropolitan area. Rocky Mountain High School is very similar to Longmont. Mount Everett is a regional high school serving five small rural New England towns. Enrollments ranged from about 250 to over 1500 students, with a median enrollment of about 1000 students. Most high schools in the United States and Canada are similar to these eight high schools.

2. Can students cope with the macro classes?

Macroclasses ranged from 3 hours and 20 minutes at West Carteret, two and a half hours at L.V. Rogers, 100 and 118 minutes at Masconomet, 95 minutes at Chelsea, and 90 minutes at Mount Everett, Longmont, Rocky Mountain, and Green River. The Harvard evaluation found that students can function effectively in macroclasses. The experience of these seven high schools strongly supports that finding. The best measure of the ability of students to handle a macroclass rests in the student conduct and the students' academic success data. If more students — or even the same proportion of students, had found the macroclasses too long and boring than those under a traditional schedule, then the documented improvements in school conduct and climate and the improvements in academic mastery would simply not have occurred. The statistical significance of the improvements experienced by these schools strongly reinforces this position.

Interestingly, the schools with the longest macroclasses seemed to have the most positive student responses. West Carteret High School's MACRO Program students, although volunteers, were very enthusiastic about their 3 hour, 20 minute classes, virtually without exception. A survey of MACRO parents got a very large return and not a single negative comment. The program was able to expand rapidly on the basis of this success. L.V. Rogers Secondary School's questionnaire results were remarkably positive, and these surveys reflected the experience of a whole school. At Chelsea a number of students were reported as complaining about their "boring" 95 minute classes. However, the results in terms of student performance at Chelsea are excellent and this reflects performance by all the students.

3. *Staff Preparation and the Copernican Programs*

The level of staff development and preparation varied greatly from school to school. However, at Masconomet and at all seven of the other schools, the basic curriculum did not change; the teachers were able to concentrate on instruction, on how to teach rather than on what to teach.

West Carteret's MACRO teachers had time to plan their change to 3 hour and 20 minute classes. A three day work shop, five half day workshops, and several smaller workshops helped prepare the staff. Some staff noted that what they learned was not always new; the difference was that they could implement it in the macroclasses while they could not under the traditional schedule. This experience paralleled Masconomet's experience.

The L.V. Rogers High School teachers had no special staff development program other than that which is normally available each year. Teachers were given small stipends to work over the summer to adapt their instruction to the Horizontal Timetable. The teachers were very much involved in the decision to try the Horizontal Timetable and in the spring, a strong majority voted to change the entire school structure the following September. The remarkable results achieved by L.V. Rogers indicates that the teachers were ready. But they were probably ready to teach those 2 1/2 hour classes long before they took that vote. Why? Under the previous traditional program, all L.V. Rogers teachers taught a minority of their classes in double, 90 minute periods, and had done so for several years. L.V. Rogers teachers were moving up from the macroclass that most the other Copernican schools are moving to. Thus, the shift to a 2 1/2 hour class was probably greatly facilitated by this prior experience with macroclasses.

The state grant awarded to the Mount Everett Regional School helped that staff plan and prepare for a significant change. The Longmont and Rocky Mountain staffs had multiyear planning processes and staff preparation programs which helped them to restructure, but they relied on local resources, not grants.

The experience of the other two high schools, Chelsea and Green River High Schools, presents a mind boggling paradox concerning the process for initiating change, and therein may be an important insight into the change process.

The school with what appeared to be one of the strongest formal staff development programs was Green River. And their commitment to staff development had been supported for many years. The Copernican change was initiated very deliberately with planning and preparation spread over a two year period. Yet based upon student performance data, its results, though positive, were clearly not at the levels of the other six schools. This information is shown in Exhibit 21, presented on the following page, which ranks these seven schools on the five evaluative factors used in this study.

Exhibit 21
A Comparison of the Impacts of Different Copernican Models Based Upon Student Performance Evaluative Data

High School	Copernican Factor				Student Performance Data											
	STD's	TCHR	Total	Rank	Improved Attend		Reductions in Suspensions		Reduced Dropouts		Greater Mastery Grades		Greater Mastery Credits		Composite	
					%	Rank	%	Rank	%	Rank	%	Rank	%	Rank	Total	Rank
L. V. Rogers	2	2	4	1	6%	1.3	-25%	4	-63%	1	6.5%	1	3.8%	6	13.3	1.5
Chelsea	3	2	5	2	6%	1.3	-75%	1	-36%	4	0.4%	6	45.6%	1	13.3	1.5
Mt. Everett	3	2.5	5.5	3	0%	5	11%	5	-33%	5	4.1%	3	13.3%	5	23.0	5
W. Carteret	3.5	3	6.5	4	6%	1.3	*	6.5	-58%	2	6.2%	2	18.5%	3	14.8	3
Longmont	4	3	7	5.5	-2%	6	*	6.5	62%	7	2.5%	4	15.5%	4	27.5	6
Rocky Mountain	4	3	7	5.5	1%	4	-38%	3	-43%	3	1.4%	5	20.0%	2	17.0	4
Green River	8	6	14	7	-9%	7	-57%	2	-17%	6	-0.5%	7	0.2%	7	29.0	7

*This data was unavailable at this school.

A summary of the meaning of this data.

1. The correlation between the rankings on the Copernican factor and the composite ranking on student performance is significant : P<0.05. If there was no relationship between these two measures, the odds are less than one in twenty that these results could occur by chance.

2. The above table provides 33 comparisons of students performance data. A total of 27 comparisons favored the Copernican schedule; 1 showed no change; 5 favored the traditional schedule. Applying the sign test, students performed significantly better under a Copernican schedule: P<.0001 sig.. This means that, if there was no relationship between the Copernican schedules and these measures of student performance, the odds are less than one in 10,000 that these results would occur by chance.

Exhibit 21 also shows that on the other extreme is Chelsea which, due to the harsh fiscal crisis, broke every rule and assumption currently comprising the conventional wisdom concerning how to change schools. Theoretically, if you had wanted to "do it wrong", you could hardly have improved on the process at Chelsea! No teacher involvement, no staff development, a reduction of over a third of the teaching staff and all staff "pink slipped". No involvement of students and the community. Yet, Exhibit 21 shows its results in terms of improved student outcomes were tied for the best record among these seven high schools. Why? What are the dynamics operating here?

There appear to be several reasons to consider. First, the Copernican Plan is based on "systemic change", a concept which permeates our current lexicon of educational "buzz words" but a concept which is ill defined and honored more in the breach than in practice. The Copernican change is truly systemic. It impacts every student, every teacher, in every class, and every day throughout the school year. It impacts on two keys to better instruction: the relationship between students and teachers and the workloads of students and teachers.

The best staff development program impacts only on teachers and can impact students only to the extent the teachers actually are able to implement what they learned, correctly and consistently, in their teaching. And under the traditional structure, that does not happen.[36] Furthermore, with rare exceptions, these staff development programs impact only a portion of the staff. Participation is usually voluntary, and those that volunteer may not be those that could profit most from what is being advocated in the staff development program. It is not systemic, because it can not impact virtually all students and teachers in every class on every day.

W. Edward Deming, the person most responsible for what is sometimes called the Japanese industrial miracle and who is the conceptual fountainhead for the Total Quality Management movement now impacting American industry and education, refers to the "85/15 rule".[37] When an organization is having problems, very often those in charge look for some one to blame: the staff, workers and administrators are considered the sources of the problems. Deming's experience is that 85% of the problems encountered by an organization are problems with the system while only 15% of an organization's problems are created by its people or subgroups. Improve the system and you solve most of the problems and the organization can then better handle the 15% of the problems which are rooted in individuals or subgroups. It follows that systemic improvements which help all the students and teachers would be far more powerful and would account for much more change than non systemic efforts that concentrate on improving the performance of part of the staff.

What is the relative power of systemic change in the Copernican models at Chelsea and Green River? Exhibit 21 presents the high schools in the order of their respective Copernican Factors, the sum of the number of classes each student attends and each teacher teaches each day. Then eachschool's student performance data are shown and each school is ranked, 1 to 7, on each set of data. The lowest score is the best student performance in this ranking. Chelsea's Copernican Factor is 5, second lowest; Green River's is 14, the highest and by quite a margin. Chelsea ties for first in change in student performance measures; Green River ranks last.

The logical explanation: staff development cannot significantly impact instructional outcomes if the basic system impedes effective implementation. Conversely, the positive power of fundamentally sound systemic change can offset the negative impacts of serious lack of participatory process, staff development and community and staff preparation.

One might conclude from the Chelsea/Green River comparison that staff development and process does not matter. This would be a major misreading of the data. Exhibit 21 shows that only 0.4 of 1% of Chelsea's improvement in mastery came from improved grades, a very small improvement. Green River's mastery based upon grades declined about 0.5 of 1%. In contrast, L.V. Rogers' teaching staff had many years of teaching 90 minute classes, and the total of 11% improvement in mastery was accounted for entirely in better student performance resulting from a major increase in higher grades and a 50% reduction in the percent of failures. Similarly, 6.2% of West Carteret's increase in mastery came from improved grades, large increases in the percentage of A's and a 50% reduction in failures. It is reasonable to anticipate at least a 5% to 10% further improvements in mastery measures if Chelsea was able to institute a strong staff development program because they have a structure which will allow the teachers to implement what they learn.

Conversely, the impact of Green River's fine staff development program could result in similar improvements in estimates of mastery if they would significantly lower their Copernican Factor. Changing the structure will allow strong staff development programs to be effective. Improvements of 10% to 15% in mastery are possible and would be significant, indeed.

4. *What Copernican model is most effective?*

There are considerable variations in the models presented in this study. Which model is most effective? That question must be answered by the students in terms of their conduct and academic performances. Once again, nothing has happened in education until it happens to a student. What is the message from the students?

Exhibit 21 compares the results obtained in each of these models in terms of student performance factors. Exhibit 21 correlates the rankings of these seven school's Copernican Factors with their composite total rankings on five student performance measures and finds the correlation is significant at the 5% level of confidence. Stated another way, if there were really no relationship between these seven school's Copernican Factors and their composite rankings, the odds on getting this type of distribution are less than one in twenty samples. These data strongly support those models with a lower Copernican factor: L.V. Rogers' Horizontal Timetable with two classes for a quarter of the year for teachers and students; Chelsea's Trimester of three classes for students and two for teachers for a third of a year, which supports Masconomet's carefully evaluated success. The long 3 hour, 20 minute classes at West Carteret had an immense impact on that school and represented a higher level of concentration than any other macroclass presented in this study. It is clear from Green River's experience that just moving to a longer class, while a positive move, is far less effective than models that result in Copernican factors of 5 or 4. These data strongly support models which provide longer macroclasses and also provide for teachers and students to deal with significantly fewer classes at a time.

5. *Real improvements or "The Hawthorne Effect"?*

Are these improvements in student performance a product of the "Hawthorne" effect?[38] The Hawthorne effect refers to the tendency of staff involved in experimental or new processes to become so enthusiastic with the innovation that the improved results are virtually guaranteed. It is the improved morale that is related to the improved performance more than any of the variables which are changed, eg: the change in schedule.

The industrial management research which identified the Hawthorne effect sought to improve productivity on a production line. Productivity was totally dependent on the workers on that line. But in this and all educational evaluations, the teachers' increased enthusiasm must be transmitted to the students, and it is the students' performance that determines the degree of success or failure. Certainly in the case of a school-within-a-school model with both students and teachers volunteering to participate, the Hawthorne effect has to be considered as a possible factor. This was a factor that had to be considered in the case of Masconomet. Some of the improvements could be assumed to come from increased staff and student dedication. However, the teachers and students who chose to stay with the traditional schedule also were dedicated to proving the traditional system was better. This group can be impacted by the "John Henry" effect, the tendency of staff, when faced with the threat of having to change, to attempt to prove that the old and familiar way was best. (John Henry's place in labor folklore is as a "steel driving man" who proved that a man could drive steel better than a steam drill, which by the way "broke".) On balance, the enthusiasm of both groups of teachers and students for their program of choice, Renpro or Tradpro, probably offset each other. It is unlikely that the Hawthorne affect accounted for much of the magnitude of improved performance experienced over that two year pilot program. This analysis would apply as well to West Carteret's experience since this was also a school-within-a-school format with teachers and students selecting their program.

In the cases of five of the other six high schools, there was some self selection by staff since majorities of about 70% voted to implement their respective Copernican schedules. However, there was also about 30% of the staff who voted against this change and this group can be impacted by the "John Henry" effect. Opposition to change is a major problem for schools considering restructuring.[39] A rereading of the "A Word From The School" sections shows that this minority of staff who opposed change was not always passive. My informal discussions indicated considerable opposition in several cases and some opposition in every case.

Students, although sometimes having some representation on committees, played a minor role in this decision to change and certainly did not have a choice or a vote on whether or not to change. The enthusiasm of the majority of the teachers had to be filtered through their students to get these results; and their enthusiasm could be countered by any opposition from the minority of staff that voted against change. Also, none of these schools was aware that a grade analysis was going to be utilized to evaluate their programs, since the request for this information did not come until the following school year. So grade escalation or the lowering of standards as a subliminal action to support a teacher's decision to support a Copernican change was improbable. Surely the Hawthorne effect does not appear to be much of a factor in accounting for the remarkable success of the L.V. Rogers Secondary School students on the British Columbia Provincial examinations nor that of the West Carteret Macro students' excellent performance on the North Carolina examinations.

Now let us consider Chelsea. No one could even remotely imply that the initiation of the Trimester at Chelsea was the result of enthusiastic involvement of the teachers or students. There was no opportunity for involvement, and there was open and emotional criticism of this decision by the teacher representatives and many others. Indeed, if there was any subliminal emotional reaction impacting Chelsea's Trimester, it would be the "John Henry Effect". Chelsea's successes are not explained by the Hawthorne effect.

One can only observe what happens in schools through the actions of students, and discerning the cause is often more difficult than measuring the results. However, on balance, these facts do not support the Hawthorne effect as a major factor in these evaluations. It is much more reasonable and logical that these results reflect real improvements in the conditions of teaching for teachers and the conditions of learning for students.

6. *Are these results sustainable?*

None of these programs has operated for more than three years, which limits claims to sustainability. We will know more about sustainability as each year is completed. Nonetheless, the weight of evidence is that they should be sustainable. Let us look at the facts.

It was the weight of significantly improved performance on a number of measures that caused the team from Harvard to conclude, after only two years, that any high school could initiate a Copernican schedule with the expectation of pedagogical gain. Similarly, the orders of magnitude between the improved results obtained by these schools under their respective Copernican structures and those obtained under their respective traditional structures are so great that a return to a traditional program cannot be justified professionally. All but one of these schools are in their second year under this structure and all are continuing their programs this year. There is no evidence from their experiences that the gains made are not sustainable. They all report that they are continuing to get similar results. For example, L.V. Rogers students were awarded another 16 provincial scholarships in their second year, matching that 400% increase in scholarship achieved in the first year. Chelsea maintained its 8.5% dropout rate in the second year.

The consistency of the favorable results achieved by these high schools is another reason for anticipating that the results are sustainable. Each of these schools is a separate case; none has any programatic relationships with any of the others. Yet there is a similarity in the results obtained. Exhibit 21 provides a recapitulation which sheds light on this question. Exhibit 21 makes 33 comparisons between a school's performance under its traditional Carnegie schedule and its performance in the first year under a Copernican schedule. One comparison showed no change, 27 favored the Copernican schedule and only 5 favored the traditional schedule. If there was really no difference in the impact of the traditional and the Copernican schedules on student performance, the odds of getting a 27 to 5 distribution in these results are less than 1 in 10,000. Results which are consistently replicable in a number of very different schools should be sustainable.

Finally, there are two schools that really pioneered the restructured schedule long before the Copernican Plan was drafted. Both are nontraditional schools, which may account for their programs not having much impact on practice in the mainstream public high schools. Fork Union Military Academy in Fork Union, Virginia, has had an intensive program since 1950.[40] Students take a single subject for the equivalent of five periods a day. Each subject is taught for eight weeks. The curriculum is limited and traditional. There is a short review period at the end of the year for students to concentrate on their weakest subject. About ninety percent of students go on to college. That is a successful record for almost half a century.

The High School in the Community, an alternative high school for minority students who want to concentrate on college preparation, is part of the New Haven, Connecticut, Public Schools.[41] This school uses an intensive format during the regular academic year. Most of the curriculum is macroscheduled: three hours a day, five days a week, for eight weeks, or a total of 120 hours per course. The program's approximately 200 students are all volunteers; they are about 90 percent minority students, and about 90 percent of them go on to college, including some of the nation's most competitive colleges. And it has been operating this program with great success for over 20 years.

There is every reason for a high school moving to a Copernican Schedule to expect significant improvements in student conduct and academic performance and to expect these results to continue for many years.

7. Time, Learning and the Copernican Results

Some, but not all the Copernican models provide less scheduled time to complete a class than is provided under the school's previous traditional schedule. The question of having less time to "cover" the curriculum has been a persistent concern to schools planning a Copernican restructuring. Let us put this concern in proper perspective, review the research concerning this question, and present some conclusions based upon this research.

Perspective
The conceptual baseline for considering time per course is the Carnegie Unit, a measure which evolved between 1893 with the establishment of the Committee of Ten, and 1907 when Henry Pritchard, President of the Carnegie Foundation For The Advancement of Teaching, defined it as 45 minutes per day for five days a week for the entire school year. (The school year varied from 36 to 40 weeks at that time, however.)[42] Interestingly, Pritchard made it clear that this definition was based upon better practice rather than theory and he also made it clear that the amount of work done rather than the time spent was the criterion. It appears that Mr. Pritchard recognized the importance of what we now refer to as "mastery learning" or "outcome based education" almost a century ago. It is good that this concept is being rediscovered!

Those who raise the question of coverage and scheduled time are usually unaware of the substantial differences in scheduled time per class that now exist, unchallenged, under the present traditional schedule. The Carnegie Unit, based upon today's 180 day school year, provides a scheduled time per class of 135 hours. By comparison, Chelsea's traditional schedule provides a 42 minute class or 126 hours per class, 7% less than the Carnegie Unit. However, Masconomet provided 46 minute classes or 139 hours per class or 10% more than Chelsea. Green River provided 50 minute classes or 150 hours per class or 20% more than Chelsea. And there are high schools with 40 minute classes, which provide 120 hours per class, and some that provide 55 minutes or 165 hours per class, a 37% difference. And often, all these differences, accompanied by different graduation requirements, coexist in high schools in the same state; indeed, within the same school district! Yet the courses offered are similarly described in each school (Algebra I; English 2; Biology; U.S.History, etc.). The curriculum to be "covered" is usually based on a text which is not classified by the hours provided to complete a course and are used by "40 minute" high schools and "55 minute" high schools. The academic equality of credits earned is almost never debated by colleges which accept them as one of a number of factors (including SAT's and ACT's) to be considered in selecting students for admission. Clearly, the Carnegie Unit as a standard is honored more in the breach than in practice.

How is the length of classes and thus, the time allowed to complete a course of study, determined? Rationally, via research concerning how time relates to how students learn, how time relates to instructional strategies shown to be most effective, or how time relates to measures of mastery? No way! Sometimes time per credit is set by the state, in which case state departments of education tend to analyze current practice within their state. However, in most schools, the length of the period is determined through collective bargaining and the decision becomes imbedded via the district's teacher contract. Usually, a maximum number of minutes of teaching per day and a maximum number of teaching assignments per day are negotiated. A maximum of 225 minutes of teaching and five teaching assignments per day equals the Carnegie Unit of 45 minutes. Based upon my observations, the teacher time available for instruction in different districts varies from 200 to 300 minutes per day, a 50% variation, and the differences between districts are usually accounted for by different "trade offs" during their respective negotiations.

The basic problem is one of a double standard. The question of coverage is raised only when there is a proposal to change the schedule, to restructure. Existing practice is assumed to be logical and is not challenged. The need to break from the conceptual bind of this century-old, "nonstandard" Carnegie Unit and the current politicized practice is critical if successful restructuring is to be achieved.

Research on Instructional Time and Learning

Fortunately, in the 87 years since Mr. Pritchard created the Carnegie Unit, there is some substantial research and solidly evaluated instructional experience concerning time and instruction which should be studied and firmly reflected in the structure of all our high schools. The following findings are taken from the research on time and learning.[43]

"The typical correlation between amount of instruction and achievement is about .40 to .50, a correlation that leaves sufficient room for other effects, but that is comparatively long and consistent."

There appears to be some surface validity in the assumption that more is learned if more time is scheduled for a class. But a correlation of .4 to .5 indicates that only 16% to 25% of the variance in student academic performance is explained by this factor. What "other effects" need to be considered? These answers are found in research on "Days of Instruction and Hours of Classes".

Days of Instruction: "The time variables in the range of days of instruction demonstrates a less consistent relationship to outcomes."

This is not the critical variable determining student performance. Classes do not necessarily have to run for 180 days.

Hours of classes: "When relationships were analyzed by amount of variance explained, the proportion ranged from 3 percent to 22 percent,"

Clearly, this also is not the most critical variable. Logically, factors other than hours per class explain the remaining 80 to 90 percent of the variance. Study time, homework time, and satisfaction level are listed as important variables.

"The time spent in class, for example, is not as closely related to achievement as is time-on-task."

It is not the time scheduled but the way the available time is used by students that is more related to achievement. Again, nothing has happened in education until it happens to a student.

"Keeping students on task requires insight or empathy that many teachers have not yet mastered."

The question this finding raises is whether a teacher is more likely to gain insight or develop empathy when dealing with five classes and about 125 students each day in classes of only 45 minutes, or whether these insights and empathy are more likely to occur if teachers deal with one, four-hour class of 25 students or two, two-hour classes and a total of 50 students each day, or some other schedule with a low Copernican Factor?

"Learning depends on how the available time is spent. Learning by the less able pupil is especially hampered by larger amounts of dead time, when nothing instructional is happening."

This finding has a particular significance for programs serving the less able student. How well is time used in our high schools?

"There is evidence that large quantities of time are dissipated in the typical classroom. —— as much as 25 percent is lost in classrooms showing good gains and 50 percent in those with poor achievement gains."

Studies show that about 40% of the time in a high school is not available for instruction and that the schedule is a major contributor to this inefficiency.[44]

The bottom line is that the time wasted under a traditional structure is so great that a more efficient structure can easily get equivalent or better results in significantly less scheduled time. And this is true of schools getting good results, as "good" is now defined under the traditional schedule.

Is there practical experience which supports this research? There is. The Harvard evaluation of the Renaissance Program found:

"Renpro students had significantly fewer hours of class (100 v. 139 hours in the first year: 118 vs. 139 hours in the second year, and 118 vs. 162 hours for science with the traditional laboratory period). While there were differences in scores between students in the two programs, these differences essentially balanced out. The results were comparable, even though there were significant differences in 'time on task.' In addition, Renpro students had more opportunities for academic enrichment (more courses, seminars, independent studies and FLEP programs) than did the Tradpro, and actually completed 13% more course credits than did Tradpro students" (pp.45-46).

The Renpro teachers constantly commented on the "flow" of the class, how easily they could move from one concept to the next and from one strategy or instructional approach to another, and how well they got to know their students and the different ways they involved their students in their own education. All of these gains came from the Copernican schedule. These Renaissance Program results are confirmed in the success achieved by Chelsea, which was also a Trimester school with less time per course.

The research cited above is further supported by the results of a most significant instructional research program. For about 25 years, Johns Hopkins University has been studying the education of very talented students. Typically, junior high school students participating in the Hopkins program complete advanced high school courses in classes which meet five hours each day, five days per week, for three weeks: a total of 75 hours, about 55% of the time allocated to these classes at a typical high school, assuming no double periods for labs. All students are pretested and post tested on well established tests eg: the College Boards achievement tests. The academic progress of the students has been exceptional. "Burn out" has not been a problem. The courses taught on the Hopkins schedule include most of the courses taught in a typical high school: English, mathematics, science, social studies, foreign languages, and humanities. The findings of follow up studies on these students are quite positive. This successful experience has also been confirmed with talented students who met a lower entrance requirement, including urban minority students.[45]

All of this evaluated experience has a common denominator. All had significantly less scheduled time than is provided in a traditional high school schedule. All have achieved significant improvements in the education of students over that achieved in traditionally scheduled programs. Why? Because, reflecting this and other research, a Copernican structure allows for significantly better use of time and establishes conditions under which practices which have been shown by research to be more effective can be implemented on a regular basis.

Conclusions

A reasonable conclusion from the experience of these schools and programs is that a Copernican structure can achieve results fully equal to and usually better than those achieved under traditional structures and do this in 20% to 25% less scheduled time, because time can be used so much more effectively. The median improvement in mastery, shown in Exhibit 21, is 18% which compares well with the 25% improvement in mastery projected in The Copernican Plan. Schools with lower Copernican Factors can achieve this 25% improvement in mastery. And this may well be a very conservative estimate. Considering the Johns Hopkins research, the real opportunity for improvement may be much higher, perhaps in the 35% to 45% range.

8. *Retention, Memory, and the Copernican Structure*

The question of retention has been a major impediment to high schools initiating Copernican restructuring. Again, there appears to be a certain surface validity to the idea that a person will forget twice as much in six months as he/she will in three months and that a gap of a year or more would be a pedagogical disaster. Let us examine the facts.

Retention was a major concern in the evaluation of Masconomet's Renaissance program, and the Evaluation Team found it not to be a problem. (Reported previously in section 4 of the Harvard Evaluation.) Part of this evaluation was based upon "gap testing", readministration of final examinations to students at different time intervals to measure their retention. On this measure, the Harvard Team found comparable retention by Renpro and Tradpro students.

Another very practical measure was the academic performance of students who took their next sequential course after a gap of six months, nine months, or a year or more. The schools included in this study are not encountering problems with retention, which parallels the experience of Masconomet's Renaissance Program. It should be carefully observed that this is the experience of the Fork Union Military Academy for over 40 years and of New Haven's High School In The Community for over 20 years. It is also the experience reported by schools using nontraditional schedules in a 1976 study of time and learning.[46] If there is some greater loss over the longer period between sequential classes, it does not appear to be great enough to be instructionally significant. But why is that true? Again, let us review the research.

A very basic research finding is that most of what is forgotten is lost in the first few weeks after it is learned. More is forgotten later, but the loss is at a very much slower rate.[47] Thus, what is forgotten over three months in the summer is not that much less than what may be forgotten over six months or a longer period of time. The Harvard Team's "gap test" findings were predicted by this research.

There are other important findings relating to retention coming from the area of cognitive psychology. If students are to retain what they are taught, educators must be concerned with students' long-term memory. After all, students will eventually leave school and it is the knowledge retained in long term memory that will allow them to use what they learned in different situations and contexts, help them in researching an answer, and make relearning relatively fast and easy. To improve long term memory, it is important that students acquire information in a well-organized manner.[48] Storing an idea for simple recognition (for example, a multiple-choice test) appears to require only a few seconds of short-term memory, but storage for production, which requires individuals to search for ideas on their own initiative (for example, an essay question or complex problem), requires about ten times as long.[49] The key lies in how information is presented. "The richness and strength of an idea in long-term memory depend largely on two principles—frequency and contiguity. The more often we encounter a particular kind of experience, the richer its representation in memory; the more closely two experiences occur in time and space, the greater the likelihood the arousal of one idea will evoke the other".[50]

These researchers refer to "chunks of knowledge" and emphasize the relatedness of facts and concepts and patterns of knowledge. "The learner must be engaged with each chunk for a reasonable amount of time, and the learner must experience several variations of the information".[51] "Why do we forget information that was once recallable? The principal answer to that question is that access to information in memory is subject to interference from competing information in memory."[52] "One of the dominant themes in contemporary memory research is that memory benefits to the extent that the material is processed for meaning."[53] Most important, when dealing with more complex "production tasks", the key to success "is not a stronger memory but a better organized one".[54]

Educators usually speak of learning and retention as separate phenomena, but according to cognitive psychologists that appears not to be so. If a person is presented with well-organized material in conditions that allow for a high level of individual attention, he or she will learn well, and what is learned well goes into long-term memory in an organized manner. As a result, it can be recalled more easily. Teaching under a traditional schedule, with students flipping from one subject to another every 45 minutes—with little chance for interaction with teachers or peers, functioning in a passive, lecture oriented instructional environment—will not provide the conditions recommended by the cognitive psychologist. Contrast that traditional class with one in which the teacher will be able to concentrate on organizing material for individuals and smaller groups of students. The Harvard Evaluation Team found 100% more group activities were used by the Renpro team than were used by their compatriots in the Tradpro. (Attachment A, p. 20) The Renpro teachers did not credit that difference to their knowing more about teaching than did their Tradpro Colleagues but rather to being able to use what they knew about better instruction. (Attachment A: pp. 19, 20, 47, 87-88) Thus a greater variety of teaching strategies can provide the several variations of different "chunks" of knowledge and other conditions recommended by this research.

The research on retention supports the position that more knowledge should be retained in long term memory under a Copernican structure. Because the teacher concentrates on fewer classes and less subject matter and can vary teaching strategies more, the probability that knowledge will be learned in a better organized fashion is greatly increased.

9. *Successful Change Must Be Research Based*

Previously I discussed Dr. Deming's 85/15 rule; 85% of the problems are in the system and only 15% are in the people or subgroups. A Copernican change is systemic; it impacts all of the students and teachers in every class and on every day. However, the traditional schedule is also systemic. It also affects every student and every teacher in every class on every day of the school year. The difference: No research supports continuing with the Carnegie unit; it actually impairs effective instruction. The Copernican structure is research based and fosters more effective instruction.

The change process must be centered on the research and supported by research based evaluations of programs that can demonstrate improved student performance.

10. *Improved Conduct Through Dejuvenilization*

One of the major objectives proposed in the Copernican Plan was to "dejuvenilize" the high school experience;[55] to treat students as young adults, to place students in mature environments with teachers who have workloads and classroom conditions that will allow them to become role models, to achieve the close relationship which is now seldom achieved and then usually by coaches and sponsors of activities. Improved student/teacher relationships were projected and it was expected that if these were achieved, they would foster incentives for better conduct which would translate into better academic performances. The major surprise from this evaluation is that these relationships were far more effective than anticipated. The impact on student conduct measures was most significant. Exhibit 21 summarizes these results.

The impact on attendance was not spectacular but it was positive, with four schools showing improved attendance, two showing declines, and one with no change. However, the startling changes occurred in the reduction of suspension rates and dropout rates. Exhibit 21 shows that four of the five high schools that were able to provide suspension data reduced suspensions from 25% to 75% during the first year under a Copernican structure; one school reported an 11% increase in suspensions.

The most significant improvement occurred in the reduction in dropout rates. Six of the seven high schools reported reductions in dropout rates ranging from 17% to 63%; Three of these high schools had serious retention problems: L.V. Rogers, Chelsea, and West Carteret. These schools had low Copernican Factors, were on quarter and trimester plans and had the longest classes of the schools in this study. The median change for the seven high schools (Chelsea High School) was 36%. As reported previously, a dropout reduction program in Massachusetts reported an 11% reduction after three years. High schools can expect to reduce dropouts and retain more students through high school graduation under a Copernican structure. Schools with large numbers of transient students will benefit from the ability to start students in classes three or four times a year and this factor alone should increase retention significantly for these at risk students.

In summation, a beneficial impact of the change to a Copernican structure is creating a dejuvenilized school climate which helps at-risk students to feel part of their classes, to know their teachers, and to experience success which results in major improvements in student conduct.

11. *Curriculum Development and the Copernican Experience*

The term curriculum development really refers to three functions: Deciding what is to be taught, its scope and sequence, which is properly defined as curriculum; suggesting how the curriculum is to be taught, which is properly defined as instruction; and finally, recommending the physical and psychological environment which will support effective instruction, which is properly defined as structure. Traditionally, the emphasis is clearly on the curriculum with some suggestions on how the curriculum might be taught, but there has been little or no consideration of the structure, the environment in which instruction must occur.[56]

In the light of the Copernican experience, I find the traditional practice of curriculum development "standing on its head", if you will. This experience tells us that our first efforts should be to give teachers and students an efficient structure, an environment in which they can work together productively. Then we should emphasize instructional development of the teaching staff so that they can use this productive environment most effectively. Then we can examine what we wish to teach, its scope and sequence, with a confident expectation that it can be taught and will be learned effectively.

A critic might take the position that there should be a relationship between curriculum, instruction, and structure; thus these three phases should be done concurrently. I agree. But the foundation of successful instruction is establishing conditions in the classroom in which teachers and students can function effectively, and this is the part of the process which is neglected. We too often are trying to build the curriculum house from the chimney down.

12. *Process Is Not Product*

Two of the seven schools evaluated in this study followed more traditional practices in achieving change. Nonetheless, both significantly improved the performances of their students. Only two schools had special grants to develop their programs. Five schools had only the normal district resources. Five of the seven schools had a solid majority of teachers supporting the proposed change; but two did not, and this was true at Masconomet as well. Yet the results at these two schools were among the best of this group. And all seven of these schools achieved significant improvements in the performances of their students. (And frankly, one is hard pressed to find evidence of even modestly improved student outcomes as a result of other current efforts at educational reform.[57])

The difference between these seven schools and many other high schools considering restructuring appears to be that change in all of these schools was far more product dominated than is usually the case, and this emphasis directed the process. Based on conversations over many years with many hundreds of educators from schools planning to change, far too often the change process itself dominates the scene, and there is an assumption that if a certain process is followed, somehow the result will be a significantly improved educational program. This assumption is neither logical nor has it been demonstrated. In all candor, I have encountered schools in which it appeared that school staff found the process useful as a means to delay change. Note carefully: process is not product.

13. *The Importance of Teachers*

In the folklore of our nation, teachers were treated with the reverence usually reserved for the clergy. But in recent decades, this reverence is reserved for the "good teacher", and underlying the rhetoric is a subliminal questioning of the effectiveness of teachers as a group, as a profession. The public really wants teachers to be successful because that will help our children to be more successful; conversely, if the public perceives that our children are not successful in school, they question the effectiveness of public schools as an institution and become concerned with the quality of instruction and the skill of our teachers.

To address this question, empowering teachers has become a major objective of the current school reform movement. But empowerment is only vaguely defined. These Copernican results were achieved simply by providing teachers with an instructional environment which allows them to practice their profession properly and provides them with students who also have more manageable workloads. Considering the results achieved, that may be a good working definition of empowerment.

The non academic gains in attendance, improved conduct, and fewer dropouts provide a special insight into the quality of the teaching under a Copernican structure. The concept of a teacher as a "role model", a concept virtually absent from the current discourse concerning secondary schools and their problems, seems to have reemerged when the teacher deals with much fewer students for much longer periods of time. A simple but major message from this research is that teachers can be immensely effective if given an opportunity to show what they can do. Even under adverse conditions in Chelsea, the majority of teachers came through for their students. Every favorable outcome reported herein is evidence of the potential effectiveness of teachers and is a tribute to their importance.

14. *Evaluate*

The major problem with most plans to change schools is the failure to plan the evaluation as an integral part of the program and to evaluate in terms of student outcomes. Whenever a new program is planned, those leading it must ask the simple question: how will we know if we are really successful? If at all possible, use competent outside evaluators. If funding is a problem, perhaps several schools could plan together and share evaluation expenses. Outside evaluators provide professional expertise not readily available in most schools. Also, they have more public credibility because they are not part of the school's administrative structure and therefore appear to be more objective. Change always generates critics. In a couple of years, critics will be looking for "solid data" and lacking this, the program could well be terminated, and the residue could well be much more "heat" than "light".

Many good professionals will advise administrators and planning teams not to initiate academic evaluations until the new program is being implemented properly, which could take several years. Our experience does not support that position. New programs should be planned well enough so that there is reason to expect some improvement. It is important to realize that the key political and professional question is whether a proposed new program is improving the education of students, based on the measures which the profession and the public will accept as "solid". Be prepared to answer that question. Again, nothing, absolutely nothing has happened in education until it has happened to a student. Evaluate!

✺   ✺   ✺   ✺   ✺   ✺   ✺

The bottomline is that the Harvard Team was right: Any school can adopt a Copernican Schedule with the expectation of pedagogical gain. One of the surprises of this research is the major improvement in conduct and attitude reflected in the three student conduct measures. While improvements were expected, improvements at these orders of magnitude were not. Also, the levels of success on all five measures are far greater and the range of success much broader than those demonstrated by any other educational reform of which the author is aware; the power of this change is truly Copernican. It is time for an educational Copernican revolution, and the opportunity is at hand.

Part IV

A Copernican Revolution For Our High Schools

"In practical matters the end is not mere speculative knowledge of what is to be done, but rather the doing of it"[58]

Aristotle

A ristotle said it correctly about 2300 years ago. Changing is a practical matter and the end is "not mere speculative knowledge of what is to be done, but rather the doing of it". **While it is possible to change without improving, it is impossible to improve without changing!**

But what is the record of the nation's high schools concerning change. Not very good.[59] Probably only one to two percent of our nation's 20,000 high schools are actively considering change and the best evidence is that very few have made much progress, particularly if one looks for evidence of change in terms of student performance. Unfortunately, this is a decades old story.

In 1983, in the original Copernican Plan concept paper, I made the following observations in response to the severe and growing criticism of our nation's schools which peaked in A NATION AT RISK: "This report forcefully challenges each local school district to meet its national responsibilities. It leaves unstated, but clearly implied, the spectral question: what if a large majority of the 15,000 school systems fail to meet this challenge: Can the Nation accept failure of such a basic, vital function as education? If this occurs, it will inevitably raise the question of whether the solution is to shift more control to the National and State level."[60]

In 1989, in THE COPERNICAN PLAN: Restructuring The American High School, I again addressed this question in a caveat: "The basic question for most educators will be "Do we really have to change?" No individual teacher or school has to change, but there is no question that this nation's high schools are going to be changed. As major national reports on education have clearly stated, the nation faces very serious problems if it cannot improve the capability of its citizenry and the quality of its work force. Will the public schools as they are now constituted make the changes necessary to achieve these goals? Or will others make the changes and create new structures to replace or drastically modify our schools? The stakes are high. As President Kennedy once said: 'If not us, who? If not now, when?' The ball is in the educators'' court."[61]

Frankly, American secondary education has not changed much even since 1983, much less since 1989. This inability to change has consequences. Many states have passed "choice" legislation, and some states include provisions for "charter schools" as well. We now have for-profit companies prepared to take over management of schools, groups of schools, and even an entire school district. Universities can also manage schools, as the Boston University/Chelsea contract demonstrates. Indeed, some have argued that the present structure for providing education is as technologically obsolete as the horse was to the automobile, and will be replaced by new systems centered around a new information highway based on rapidly expanding, microchip based technology. And much of the technology is already available. Some who oppose change seem to paraphrase President Eisenhower's famous admonition: "Beware of the educational/industrial complex." But if the present system can not demonstrate that it can meet the nation's needs satisfactorily, can it stand in the path of other options? I think not.

It surely is time to quit speculating and to take action. Indeed, the time is late. In the following sections, we will consider how implementation of the Copernican Plan is related to achievement of our nation's educational goals and how the nation's high schools could take the lead in a much needed educational revolution.

NATIONAL GOALS AND COPERNICAN OPPORTUNITIES

Assuming every high school in the nation, over 20,000 schools, shifted from a Carnegie based structure to a Copernican structure, would it make much difference in our nation's ability to meet major national demands for improved student performance? To respond to this question, the national goals must be identified. Consider first the goals set forth in 1990 by President Bush and the Nation's governors in a document entitled: America 2000 An Education Strategy.[62] President Clinton was a member of the governors' group that helped draft these goals, and they have been retained by his administration. While the strategies for achieving these six goals generate considerable controversy, the goals themselves are fairly well accepted. The first goal is concerned with a child's readiness for school, which I consider to be the most important goal, but it is not one impacted by the Copernican Plan. Let us consider the other five goals:

Goal 2: The America 2000 strategy proposed that the high school graduation rate increase to at least 90%.

This goal presumes a problem with the present graduation rate. What is the present graduation rate? There are different approaches to determine dropout rates based on different assumptions and for different purposes.[63] Three measures are utilized: event rates, status rates, and cohort rates. What measures should high schools use? Let us consider these measures briefly. Event rates are based upon the number of students who drop out in a single year without completing high school. Event rates are the basis for state dropout reports and are the dropout rates used in Part Two of this book. Status rates measure the portion of a particular population (eg. 16 through 24 years of age) who have not completed high school and who are not enrolled in school at a particular time. Status rates are derived from U.S.Census data and are useful in reflecting the impact of GED and adult education programs. Cohort rates measure what happens to a single group (or cohort) of students over a period of time. They record the total dropouts from a class or cohort over several years. This is the approach which is appropriate in measuring the impact of k-12 programs and particularly of high school programs.

In using the cohort rates, questions need to be answered concerning the cohort used. Should we measure the dropouts beginning with eighth grade, the ninth grade, or the tenth grade? Whatever the grade with which we begin, should we end the measurement at enrollment in the twelfth grade, at actual high school graduation, or sometime after graduation in order to account for those who may have been delayed in completing all their graduation requirements.

It is not clear which of these measures of dropouts was in mind when the "90%" goal was set. However, a task force of the Council of Chief State School Officers describes a dropout as: "A pupil who leaves school, for any reason except death, before graduation or completion of a program of studies and without transferring to another school".[64] Credits for high school graduation begin in the ninth grade. Clearly, for those people concerned with improving our high schools, the appropriate measure is the percentage of ninth grade students that continue through to graduation in the twelfth grade or earlier.

This ninth grade to high school graduation information is reported every year by the U.S. Office of Education.[65] For perspective, the graduation rates increased from 57.9% in 1939-40, when reporting began, to 78.5% in 1968-69, the highest retention rate reported through 1990-91, the last year for which information is available. It is clear that a 90% graduation rate is not a return to some previous standard but is a new, much higher standard deemed necessary for our work force to be internationally competitive.

In the last decade for which information was available, high school retention of students through graduation declined slightly from 72.1% in 1980-81 to 71.2% in 1990-91; the highest retention rate reported for these years was 73.9%, so the retention rate has been very stable. The problem is more difficult if viewed from the position of individual states. For example in 1990-91, retention rates in the 50 states and the District of Columbia ranged from 54.3% to 89.5%. And the problem is grim in the large cities where up to half of all students entering ninth grade fail to graduate four years later.[66] And this record was compiled during a decade when the retention of students in school has been of great concern and was the subject of legislative concern; a number of states have initiated dropout prevention programs. We have a long way to go to meet this goal of 90% retention, and there is no evidence of progress to date.

Implementing Copernican structures can make a major contribution towards achieving this goal. Six of the seven Copernican high schools in this study reduced their dropout rates from 17% to 58%, with a median reduction for the seven schools of 36%. Based upon this record, it is reasonable that the national dropout rate could be reduced from 29% (71% graduating) to 19% (81% graduating) within two or three years and with virtually no additional cost, assuming all high schools are implementing Copernican structures. Probably the reduction of dropouts would be greater if high schools adopted schedules having lower Copernican factors. In this regard, it is useful to review the position of the West Carteret High School planning team that developed the MACRO Program: "The most effective dropout deterrent is not a specialized program targeting a small sub- group but rather a more effective knowledge delivery system and an overall, pervasive change in school climate". With fuller implementation of other parts of the Copernican Plan such as seminars, use of the flexibility of the schedule to support apprenticeships and community service programs, Individualized Learning Plans and other measures that would dejuvenilize the high school experience, it seems reasonable that the nation's graduation rate could be closer to the 90% target. **Just change the system.**

Goal 3: Goal 3 should be considered in two parts. First, the America 2000 strategy proposes that students will leave grade 12 "having demonstrated competency in challenging subjects including English, mathematics, science, history, and geography".

This goal should be viewed in the context of Goal 2 to graduate 90% of our students. Goal 2's objective is not to just keep more students in school for more years; it is to keep them in school in order to significantly improve their academic competency. Goal 3 requires improved competency for all students.

Six of the seven of the Copernican high schools improved academic mastery by 6% to 46%, as measured in higher grades and the numbers of courses successfully completed; one school showed no change. The median was an 18% increase in mastery. If the Copernican schedules selected provide for a low Copernican factor, this improvement in mastery should be in the 25% range.

However, Goal 3 does not define "competency", and some may argue that passing a course in a typical American high school today, or even in seven Copernican American/Canadian high schools, doesn't ensure competency as intended in Goal 3. In response to that very legitimate question, the success of West Carteret High School's MACRO students on the North Carolina examinations and the success of L.V.Rogers Secondary School's students on the "high stakes", British Columbia provincial examinations supports the probability of many more students meeting what those jurisdictions consider to be good quality standards in challenging subjects. Implementing a Copernican schedule in every high school would make a major contribution towards achieving this goal. **Just change the system.**

Goal 3: The last part of Goal 3 of The America 2000 strategy proposes that "- - every school in America will ensure that all students learn to use their minds well, so they may be prepared for responsible citizenship, further learning, and productive employment in our modern economy".

The Harvard evaluation of the Renaissance Program found that students experiencing a Copernican structure developed better problem solving skills than did their peers under a traditional schedule, and the findings were statistically very significant. The Copernican Plan encourages and accommodates cooperative group instruction and more in-depth analysis of problems in every class, every day. It makes it possible for a student to deal with current issues seminars as part of the regular school program. It also has the flexibility to allow for field trips, exchanges, and community service with a minimum of disruption in other classes, all of which will make school a more "dejuvenilized" experience and can contribute to improved citizenship. These improvements in problem solving skills can be achieved by students in any high school; **just change the system.**

Goal 4: The America 2000 strategy proposes that "U.S. students will be first in the world in science and mathematics achievement".

In the context of that report, this goal proposes that all students should improve their performances, including but not limited to the higher ability students.

The United States has not fared well in international academic competitions, which prompted inclusion of this goal. The fact that the nations whose students are besting ours in academic competitions are also those which are "eating our lunch" economically adds to the urgency and political pressure behind this goal.

These international competitors have much longer school years and operate under a schedule that is similar to our nation's traditional schedules. There are many who argue for the lengthening of our school year as a means for our students to compete more effectively academically. Additional costs have been a major stumbling block to attempts to extend the school year. However, if we invested, for example, enough to extend the school year from 180 to 225 days, a 25% increase, it would be done on the assumption that learning would increase in approximately direct proportion. The research, cited above in Part Two, finds that differences in scheduled time explains only about 20% of the difference in academic performance of our students.[67] These evaluations strongly support the position that we can achieve that much improvement within the present school year. It would do little to make our students more competitive if we just add time without first addressing the question of how to make the best use of the time we now have. Once we have an efficient use of existing resources, then the movement to a longer year could be justified, and should be considered as an investment that could achieve this goal.

Certainly, the broad based increase in mastery demonstrates that the Copernican Plan establishes a structure which will result in a more competitive group of students. But no system can guarantee U.S. students will be first in the world; one major reason is that we cannot predict what all the other countries will do to improve the educational performances of their students; perhaps they will be the ones to change and improve. We should have a much better chance at coming in first than is the case today. **Again, just change the system.**

Goal 5: The America 2000 strategy proposes that "Every adult American will be literate and will possess the knowledge and skills necessary to compete in a global economy and exercise the rights and responsibilities of citizenship".

The functional illiteracy of so many of our adults, which is the reason for the inclusion of this national goal, is not limited to the high school dropout. It is a problem for many who officially graduated. Their experience shows their high school diplomas were tickets to nowhere. But these people are products of the present system, could be assisted by adult basic education programs, and would appear not to be impacted by changing present high schools to a Copernican structure. However, prevention of failure is much more desirable and efficient than remediation. To the extent that elementary and secondary schools are successful, fewer adult basic education programs are needed. The funds now used to compensate for undereducated dropouts and high school graduates could be shifted to apprenticeship programs, continuing education and life time learning, where we do have substantial needs. Prevention of failure is how a Copernican change could make a major contribution towards achieving this goal.

A national change to a Copernican Schedule should reduce dropout rates. Reducing dropouts should give our high schools a chance to reduce the numbers of functionally illiterate citizens; we cannot educate them if they aren't in school! The experience reported from many of the schools included in this study indicates that recent dropouts returned to school because they could complete courses needed for graduation in a third or a quarter of a year. Urban high schools usually deal with large numbers of transient students who usually dropout and add to the numbers of economically impaired adults. Being able to complete a course in a quarter or a third of a year, being able to begin courses with other students three or four times each year instead of always being "far" to "hopelessly" behind in five or six classes per day for the remainder of the 180 day school year, will do much to help these at-risk students to become part of their new school and achieve better. The success of these students will help the nation achieve this goal.

Having our students able to compete in a global economy was addressed above in considering goal 4. In considering the question of global competitiveness, the observations of Lester Thurow, professor and formerly Dean of M.I.T.'S Sloan School of Management and an economist and international consultant of the first order, should be carefully considered: "—when the name of the game is new processes, the key problem is educating the bottom 50 percent, because if they cannot use the new high-tech procedures, they won't be able to join the American work force."[68] These Copernican evaluations show clearly that lower performing students, students in the bottom half in academic comparisons, significantly improve their performances. There needs to be more clearly defined performance levels to meet Goal 5. Nonetheless, it is clear that meeting those higher standards and vastly improving the mastery and performance levels of the students who are now in the lower 50% academically has not occurred in the many decades under the present traditional, Carnegie based structure, and it appears unreasonable to expect much improvement. Conversely, much improved performance levels are likely to be achieved under a Copernican structure. **Just change the system.**

Goal 6: The America 2000 strategy proposes that "Every school in America will be free of drugs and violence and will offer a disciplined environment conducive to learning".

Clearly, the Copernican Plan and these evaluations did not deal with drugs, and only tangentially with violence via suspensions. However, recognizing this limitation, let us review these evaluated findings against this national goal.

The goal presents an assumption of a relationship between a more disciplined environment and reduction in usage of drugs and the incidence of violence; this is a reasonable assumption. Clearly, the Copernican structure makes a substantial contribution towards the achievement of a much more disciplined environment, and the oft cited improved academic mastery shows the resulting environment is more conducive to learning for all students, including at-risk students. Indeed, personal acceptance, daily interaction with teachers, and academic success in each class appears to reduce the frustrations that lead students to poor conduct. Specifically, five of the seven high schools had the data to report on changes in suspension rates for their schools during the first year under a Copernican structure. Four of the five had reductions in suspensions ranging from 25% to 75%; one school reporting an increase had an 11% increase. If suspensions, which are imposed in cases of more serious misconduct, are down, violence may be reduced.

However, it appears that students who commit felonious, news reportable violence are often from a hard core, small minority of students, and it may be the larger group of less violent but disruptive students whose conduct is improved by a more productive and personalized school environment. It would take more research and evaluation than has been done to date to determine if this is the case and to what extent a Copernican change would impact this hard core group. However, less violence could be a positive spinoff. But only if we **change the system.**

OPPORTUNITY FOR A COPERNICAN REVOLUTION

All that is necessary to make significant progress toward achieving these major national educational goals is for every high school in the nation to make a relatively simple Copernican change. And this change in structure should be achievable in two to three years; it should not require decades. There is no professional reason for delay; indeed, continuing the present traditional structure raises a question of professional malpractice. There is no economic reason for delay. The change in structure, the systemic change, will get significantly better results than will be possible under the traditional structure.

Implementing a Copernican structure will make present high school programs much more effective. But the potential impact is much greater. Implementation of any significant instructional change is dependent upon the Copernican change in the daily and yearly schedules. Failure to make this change from the traditional schedules will seriously impede effective implementation of promising ideas and the conversion of solidly based research into instructional practice.

For a fundamental change of virtually all of our nation's high schools, approximately 20,000 schools, to occur within a few years would be revolutionary, indeed, particularly considering the well established record of our nation's high schools' adherence to the status quo. But a revolution is coming. It will either be a revolutionary change in the responsiveness of those groups currently in control of our schools in solving our nation's educational problems, or it will be a revolution centered in instituting alternatives to the present system.

The need for our high schools to fundamentally change is real and is urgent. The critics are correct in assessing this need, and our critics include many distinguished national leaders and also a number of distinguished educators.[69] Recent studies initiated by the U. S. Office of Education find about half of our adult work force to be too poorly educated to qualify for all but the jobs requiring the lowest level work skills;[70] those jobs which usually can be automated or can be moved to third world countries most easily. There will be fewer jobs for people with these low level skills, and there will be too many people competing for them. And our more able students must be prepared to perform more ably. A significantly higher percentage of our students must be prepared to work in higher technology occupations. And all students will require a much better education to be an effective citizen in this increasingly more complex world. Indeed, they may well need to know more to be effective citizens than to be productive employees.

A Copernican revolution in secondary education is possible. We can apply our professional knowledge to make a major contribution to our country as it deals with its immensely difficult problems of economic leadership in an emerging new world order. Our high schools can be far better than they have ever been. Our national values emphasize inclusion and equal opportunity, which is part of the historic mission of our public school systems. Our form of government is dependent upon high levels of citizen support and responsibility. This proposed change reflects such values. It is predicated on implementing higher standards through greater individualization of instruction; it builds on an instructional environment that fosters concern for each student and involvement of each student. Furthermore, our high schools can make these improvements within our own system rather than copying that of another nation, by demonstrating efficiency and effectiveness in meeting our major responsibilities: the development of knowledgeable and caring citizens who are also economically competent and reliable employees.

But returning to Aristotle's dictum, the time for speculating is past; now is the time for the "doing of it". Many of our critics say the secondary schools and particularly high schools cannot change significantly. That criticism will not be put to rest by further debate but only by the actions of thousands of high school staffs and the resulting improved performances of their students. The opportunity for a Copernican revolution in secondary education is here. We can do it. And the best part is that we can do it our way. Let us get on with it!

END NOTES

1 Carroll, Joseph M. 1983. THE COPERNICAN PLAN: A Concept Paper Concerning the Restructuring of Secondary Education at the Masconomet Regional School District. Topsfield, MA. This was a 71 page concept paper which was widely circulated.

2 Bronowski, Jacob. 1973. The Ascent of Man. Boston: Little, Brown and Company. p. 197

3 American Educational Research Association. 1992. Encyclopedia of 4 Educational Research, 6th ed. New York: MacMillan. pp. 613-618.

4 Goodlad, John. 1984 A Place Called School. New York: McGraw-Hill pp. 105-106.

5 Carroll, Joseph M. 1989. The Copernican Plan: Restructuring The American high School. Andover, Massachusetts 01810: The Regional Laboratory for Educational Improvement of the Northeast and Islands. p. 15.

6 Machiavelli, Nicolo. (1469-1527) The Prince. Chapter 6 Translation by W. K. Marriott.

7 Carroll, Joseph M. 1983. THE COPERNICAN PLAN: A Concept Paper Concerning the Restructuring of Secondary Education at the Masconomet Regional School District. Topsfield, MA. Appendix III, pp. 1-17.

8 Carroll, Joseph M. 1989. The Copernican Plan: Restructuring The American high School. Andover, Massachusetts 01810: The Regional Laboratory for Educational Improvement of the Northeast and Islands. p. 27.

9 Carroll, Joseph M. 1989. The Copernican Plan: Restructuring The American high School. Andover, Massachusetts 01810: The Regional Laboratory for Educational Improvement of the Northeast and Islands. pp. 51-54.

10 American Educational Research Association. 1982. Encyclopedia of Educational Research, 5th ed. New York: MacMillan. p. 2031.

11 The Province. November 12, 1991, p. A26. A QUIET INNOVATION AT L.V. ROGERS HIGH SCHOOL IN NELSON. Nelson, British Columbia.

12 Hierck, Thomas A. and Veregin, Lawrence E. A Comparison of the Horizontal Timetable versus the Linear Timetable for a Senior Secondary School. An unpublished research completed by two teachers from the L. V. Rogers Secondary School in partial fulfillment of requirements for a Master of Arts in Administration and Curriculum at Gonzaga University, Spokane, Washington.

13 Ibid

14 Ibid p. 26.

15 Based on a letter, dated March 27, 1993, from Bill Reid, principal of the L.V. Rogers Secondary School in response to a request for information from the author. The records show a reduction of 7% in 1991-2 from 1990-91. However, in 1991-92, a new policy concerning tardiness was instituted which required students who are beginning to have attendance problems to receive a "friendly talk" with an administrator to try to reduce the occurrence of more serious problems. These "talks", however, are recorded as a disciplinary matter. Operating under the previous policy, the administration estimates a reduction of about 25%.

16 Ibid.

In response to the author's question concerning the change in suspensions, Principal Reid compared the suspension rate of the current 12th grade class when they were 10th graders and under the traditional system with that of the current 10th graders who are in their first year at Rogers and are under the Horizontal Timetable. Suspensions of the current 10th grade students was only a third of the 12th grade comparison group who began under the traditional schedule. Thus an estimate of a 25% reduction in suspensions during the first year under the Copernican type schedule is both reasonable and conservative.

17 This information was provided by Bill Reid, principal of L.V. Rogers Secondary School. It is also confirmed later in the "A Word From The School" section which was written by Bill Reid.

18 American Educational Research Association. 1982. Encyclopedia of Educational Research, 5th ed. New York: MacMillan. p. 1142.

19 Chelsea High School enrolled grades 7 to 12 in 1990-91 and grades 9 to 12 in 1991-92. Based on a written report from the Chelsea high school administration re 1990-91 and Mass. Dept. of Ed. reports for 1991-92.

20 Dropout Rates in Massachusetts Public Schools: 1991. Publication by the Massachusetts Department of Education. March 1993. p. 25.

21 This information was based on responses to this question by the following Chelsea High School administrators, all of whom held their positions in both the 1990-91 and 1991-92 school years: Principal Elsa Wasserman, Assistant Principal Andre Ravanelle, and Assistant Principal Ron Toleos.

22 Drop out rates were provide by the Massachusetts Department of Education.

23 Dropout Rates in Massachusetts Public Schools: 1991. Publication by the Massachusetts Department of Education. Quincy, Massachusetts. March 1993. p. 2.

24 Carroll, Joseph M. 1989. The Copernican Plan: Restructuring The American high School. Andover, Massachusetts 01810: The Regional Laboratory for Educational Improvement of the Northeast and Islands. pp. 31-32.

25 "The Odyssey 2000 and beyond" An unpublished description of the Mount Everett program prepared and reproduced by the school's staff.

26 Carteret County Schools proposal to the North Carolina Department of Education for inclusion in the "Governor's Programs of Excellence in Education, 1992-93. West Carteret's Macro Program was selected for statewide recognition.

27 Ibid

28 Ibid

29 This information was provided by the Green River High School administration.

30 Wyoming "Attendance and Membership" records for 1990-91 and for 1991-92 which were provided by the Registrar at Green River High School.

31 Dropout Rates in Massachusetts Public Schools: 1991. Publication by the Massachusetts Department of Education. Quincy, Massachusetts. March 1993. p. 2.

"The annual dropout rate statewide for schools targeted by (Dropout Prevention) grants was 7.8 percent, down from 8.8 percent in 1988."

32 Based on information provided by the Independence High School administration.

33 The source of this information is a report prepared by the Rutland Senior Secondary School administration entitled: PRELIMINARY SUCCESS INIDICATORS AT R.S.S.; 1991/92 & 1992/93. All of the data presented is this section are based on this document.

34 The source of all data concerning Omak High School came from the evaluative material provided by the Omak High School administration.

35 Muncey, Donna E. and McQuillan, Patrick J. Preliminary Findings from a Five-Year Study of the Coalition of Essential Schools. February 1993 PHI DELTA KAPPAN. Bloomington, Indiana. pp. 486-489.

Schmoker, Michael J. and Wilson, Richard B. 1993. TOTAL QUALITY EDUCATION: Profiles Of Schools That Demonstrate The Power Of Deming's Management Principles. Phi Delta Kappa Educational Foundation. Bloomington, Indiana. pp. xiii-ivx; 163-166.

Louis, Karen Seashore and Miles, Matthew B. 1990. IMPROVING THE URBAN HIGH SCHOOL. Teachers College Press. New York, NY. pp. 49-51.

36 Goodlad, John. 1984 A Place Called School. McGraw-Hill. New York, NY. pp. 105-106.

American Educational Research Association. 1982. Encyclopedia of Educational Research, 5th ed. New York: MacMillan. p. 1050-1051.

37 Walton, Mary. Deming Management at Work. 1990 New York, G. P. Putnam's. p. 20.

38 Dubin, Robert. Human Relations in Administration. Prentice-Hall, New York 1951. p. 326-329.

The author references and reviews the famous Hawthorne experiments, so named because they were conducted at the Western Electric Company's Hawthorne facility by F. J. Roethlisberger and W. J. Dickson of the Harvard Business School. Their research is presented in their book, Management and the Worker. Harvard University Press, 1943.

"The controlled observation of small work groups over a number of years indicated that increased production on the whole seemed more closely related to the 'morale' of the group than to any of the variables—which were tested."

39 Muncey, Donna E. and McQuillan, Patrick J. Preliminary Findings from a Five-Year Study of the Coalition of Essential Schools. February 1993 PHI DELTA KAPPAN. Bloomington, Indiana. pp. 486-489.

40 Powell, Barbara Schieffelin. 1976, Intensive Education: The Impact of Time on Learning. Newton, MA: Educational Development Center.

41 Carroll, Joseph M. 1989. The Copernican Plan: Restructuring The American high School. Andover, Massachusetts 01810: The Regional Laboratory for Educational Improvement of the Northeast and Islands. p. 51.

42 American Educational Research Association. 1950. Encyclopedia of Educational Research, 1st ed. New York: MacMillan. p. 1181.

43 American Educational Research Association. 1982. Encyclopedia of Educational Research, Fifth Ed. New York: MacMillan. pp. 917-924.

44 Rosmiller, Richard A. 1985. "Time-On-Task: A Look at What Erodes Time for instruction," The Best of the NASSP Bulletin: Readings in Secondary School Administration. Washington, DC: National Association of Secondary School Principals.

45 Durden, William C. 1987. Taped presentation to parents and faculty at Masconomet (MA) Regional School District, December 14, 1987.

The work of Johns Hopkins University's CTY program for gifted students has demonstrated that very able students successfully complete very demanding courses in a wide range of disciplines in a total of 75 hours: five hours/day for three weeks or 15 days. They have now been able to get comparable results with less talented students. If one can achieve in 75 hours what schools using a Carnegie unit allocate 135 to achieve, 45% of the students time is essentially wasted in a lockstep environment. If that time was better utilized, 80% greater learning would appear to be feasible. However, research indicates that variations in scheduled time only explains about 20% of the variations in academic achievement, so a 35% to 45% estimate may be more appropriate. If teachers were provided excellent programs concerning how to teach more effectively and had a classroom environment that allowed them to use this knowledge systemically, the academic improvements could be even greater.

46 Powell, Barbara Schieffelin. 1976. Intensive Education: The Impact of Time on Learning. Newton, MA: Educational Development Center.

47 Ebbinghaus, H. 1913. Memory (H. A. Ruger & D. E. Bussenius, Translation). N.Y.. Teachers College Press.

This is very old research. In considering this reference, note the comments regarding Ebbinhaus from the Encyclopedia of Learning and Memory. 1992. Macmillan Publishing Company, New York. pp. 153-54. Ebbinhaus "was founder of experimental psychology of memory." "Despite the pioneering nature of his work, he did just about everything right by the standards of science."

48 Calfee, Robert. 1981. "Cognitive Psychology and Educational Practice", Review of Research in Education. Washington, DC: American Educational Research Association. p. 18-19.

49 Ibid p. 20.

50 Ibid p. 20.

51 Ibid p. 40.

52 Encyclopedia of Learning and Memory. 1992. Macmillan Publishing Company. New York. p. 283.

53 Ibid p. 545.

54 Calfee, Robert. 1981. "Cognitive Psychology and Educational Practice," Review of Research in Education. Washington, DC: American Educational Research Association. p. 21.

55 Carroll, Joseph M. 1989. The Copernican Plan: Restructuring The American high School. Andover, Massachusetts 01810: The Regional Laboratory for Educational Improvement of the Northeast and Islands. pp. 45-46.

56 American Educational Research Association. 1982. Encyclopedia of Educational Research, Sixth Ed. New York: MacMillan. pp. 262-269.

"Implementation is a relatively new topic for curriculum research" The article notes that it was not even a topic in previous editions of the encyclopedia. The current research supports the role of teachers, but does begin to address the question of structure. However, I believe the predominant practice is as stated here.

57 Muncey, Donna E. and McQuillan, Patrick J. Preliminary Findings from a Five-Year Study of the Coalition of Essential Schools. February 1993 PHI DELTA KAPPAN. Bloomington, Indiana. pp. 486-489.

Schmoker, Michael J. and Wilson, Richard B. 1993. TOTAL QUALITY EDUCATION: Profiles Of Schools That Demonstrate The Power Of Deming's Management Principles. Phi Delta Kappa Educational Foundation. Bloomington, Indiana. pp. xiii-ivx; 163-166.

Louis, Karen Seashore and Miles, Matthew B. 1990. IMPROVING THE URBAN HIGH SCHOOL. Teachers College Press. New York, NY. pp.49-51.

Site-Based Management. 1991. Educational Research Service. Arlington, VA. 22201. p. 7.

58 Aristotle. Nicomachean Ethics, VI, 13, 1.

59 Muncey, Donna E. and McQuillan, Patrick J. Preliminary Findings from a Five-Year Study of the Coalition of Essential Schools. February 1993 PHI DELTA KAPPAN. Bloomington, Indiana. pp. 486-489.

Schmoker, Michael J. and Wilson, Richard B. 1993. TOTAL QUALITY EDUCATION: Profiles Of Schools That Demonstrate The Power Of Deming's Management Principles. Phi Delta Kappa Educational Foundation. Bloomington, Indiana. pp. xiii-ivx; 163-166.

Louis, Karen Seashore and Miles, Matthew B. 1990. IMPROVING THE URBAN HIGH SCHOOL. Teachers College Press. New York, NY. pp.49-51.

Site-Based Management. 1991. Educational Research Service. Arlington, VA. 22201. p. 7.

60 Carroll, Joseph M. 1983. THE COPERNICAN PLAN: A Concept Paper Concerning the Restructuring of Secondary Education at the Masconomet Regional School District. Topsfield, MA. p. 6.

61 Carroll, Joseph M. 1983. THE COPERNICAN PLAN: A Concept Paper Concerning the Restructuring of Secondary Education at the Masconomet Regional School District. Topsfield, MA. p. 89.

62 AMERICA 2000, An Educational Strategy. 1991. U.S. Department of Education. Washington D.C.. p.19.

This section addresses five of the six Goals established at the Charlottsville Education Summit, called by the Bush administration.

63 Dropout Rates in the United States: 1991. U.S. Department of Education, National Center for Education Statistics. NCES92-129 p. v

64 OERI Urban Superintendents Network. 1987. Dealing with Dropouts: The Urban Superintendents' Call to Action. Office of Educational Research and Improvement, U.S. Department of Education. Washington D.C. p. 11.

65 PUBLIC HIGH SCHOOL GRADUATES, 1990-91, COMPARED WITH 9TH GRADE ENROLLMENT IN FALL 1987, BY STATE. U.S. Department of Education, National Center for Education Statistics. Unpublished document.

This information is gathered annually, going back to 1939-40. The state information has not been adjusted for interstate migration. The national dropout figures are quite accurate but probably understate the case since there has been a steady inmigration of students particularly over the last decade, which would tend to offset the departure of some students and result in higher retention rates.

66 OERI Urban Superintendents Network. 1987. Dealing with Dropouts: The Urban Superintendents' Call to Action. Office of Educational Research and Improvement, U.S. Department of Education. Washington D.C. p. 1.

67 American Educational Research Association. 1982. Encyclopedia of Educational Research, Fifth Ed. New York: MacMillan. pp. 917-924.

68 Thurow, Lester. September 1991. The American School Board Journal. p. 43.

69 Carroll, Joseph M. 1989. The Copernican Plan: Restructuring The American high School. Andover, Massachusetts 01810: The Regional Laboratory for Educational Improvement of the Northeast and Islands. pp. 17-19.

70 Kirsch, Irwin S.: Jungeblut, Ann; Jenkins, Lynn; Kolstad, Andrew. 1993. Educational Testing Service under contract with the National Center for Educational Statistics, Office of Educational Research and Improvement, U.S. Department of Education. Washington, D.C. pp. xiii-xxi.

ATTACHMENT A

The Masconomet Regional High School Renaissance Program:

The First Implementation of the
Copernican Plan

The Final Report of the
Harvard Evaluation Team

Dean K. Whitla, Ph.D.
Janine Bempechat, Ed.D.
Vito Perrone, Ph.D.
Barbara B. Carroll, Ed.D.

May, 1992

Acknowledgements

The authors gratefully acknowledge the assistance of Gabrielle Bamford, Miya Omori and Paul Schlichtman in the data collection phases of this evaluation.

Contents

EXECUTIVE SUMMARY

In 1989, the Masconomet Regional School District instituted within the Masconomet Regional High School an experimental educational restructuring design known as the Renaissance program. This program essentially restructured the traditional use of school time to provide students with fewer classes taught in longer class periods, with each class to be completed in part of the school year, a trimester. Students attended two approximately two-hours-per-day courses per trimester. It was believed that this schedule, which allowed students to devote more time and attention to sustained inquiry into the subject matter, would result in superior learning experiences. Moreover, longer classroom periods were believed to allow teachers to create classroom cultures of collaborative group work.

During these two years, students were tested, classrooms were observed, and students, parents, teachers and administrators were surveyed and interviewed. Many comparisons were made between the Traditional program and the Renaissance program. The following are major results of the evaluation effort. **Please note that all differences reported are statistically significant, unless otherwise indicated.**

- Renaissance students were more satisfied than Traditional students with the quality of the relationships they had formed with their teachers. They reported that the small classes fostered better discussions and deeper understandings of course material.

- Parents of students in the Renaissance program were pleased with their children's increased motivation, and noted their children's improved relationships with teachers. They also noted an improvement in their children's academic performance, especially compared with their previous school record.

- Classroom observations showed that the Renaissance teachers were more innovative in their pedagogy. For example, Renaissance teachers made more use of group learning than did Traditional teachers.

- School guidance counselors observed that Renaissance students were pleased with the small classes, the fact that they could concentrate on only two courses at one time, and the closer contact with teachers.

- Department chairs were pleased with the high degree of student-teacher interaction, but were concerned about the demands the program placed on teachers.

- The academic performances of Renaissance and Traditional students were essentially equivalent. These results were achieved even though there was substantially less total class time for each course in the Renaissance program. Students who chose the Renaissance program were less able verbally and mathematically: even so, they completed more course credits than did students in the Traditional program. Tests of students' retention of subject matter showed that Renpro and Tradpro students retained material comparably. Tests administered to determine students' ability to think through problems and to work cooperatively found that Renaissance students performed significantly higher than did Traditional students. Overall, the Renaissance program appears to have met its academic objectives.

- The Renaissance program frequently encountered opposition from members of the school community not associated with the program. Such opposition, coupled with general school financial problems, resulted in the program's demise after only two basically successful and promising years.

- From a research perspective, two years of program evaluation did not provide final, conclusive answers. More research is needed. However, it is fair to conclude that a Copernican-type program can be undertaken with the expectation of pedagogical improvements, and to place the burden of proof on those supporting the Traditional program.

THE RENAISSANCE PROGRAM: A COPERNICAN PILOT PROGRAM

Joseph M. Carroll, Ed.D., Superintendent

Masconomet Regional District

The Renaissance Program was developed around the basic concepts of the Copernican Plan, which proposed that "virtually every high school in this nation can decrease its average class size by 20 percent; increase its course offerings or number of sections by 20 percent; reduce the total number of students with whom a teacher works each day by 60 to 80 percent; provide students with regularly scheduled seminars dealing with complex issues; establish a flexible, productive instructional environment that allows effective mastery learning as well as other practices recommended by educational research; get students to master 25 to 30 percent more information in addition to what they learn in the seminars; and do all of this within approximately present levels of funding" (Carroll, 1989). The effort to restructure schools focuses on two primary factors which are the major determinants of the quality of instruction: the relationships between teachers and students, and the workloads of both teachers and students.

The 1989-90 Renaissance Program

After three years of discussions of the Copernican Plan, the teachers at Masconomet created the Renaissance program. Its major goals were similar to those cited above: to improve the workload of teachers and the relationship between teachers and students, to make instruction more effective, and to initiate a seminar and independent study program. The most visible evidence of the program in the school was marked change in the daily and yearly schedules. The Renaissance Program was organized as a school-within-a-school, which served about eighty 9th grade students. It was a program of "choice": students volunteered to be in the program. The 80 students who selected the pilot program became known as "Renpro" students, and the approximately 95 students who decided to stay with the traditional program similarly became known as "Tradpro" students.

Each Renaissance student was enrolled in two 100 minute classes each day. Each class met for a trimester, or for 60 days. Thus, each class met for a total of 100 hours. Since the traditional classes met for 46 minutes a day for 181 days per year, or 139 hours, a Renaissance class met for some 28% less time.

In three trimesters, Renaissance students completed six 100 hour courses, all in the morning during the same time that Traditional students had their first four class periods. It was not economically feasible to schedule all electives separately for each program, so a number of ninth grade electives were scheduled for both programs in the afternoon: the schedule consisted of three elective 46 minute periods (the Traditional fifth, sixth and seventh periods).

In the fifth period, Renaissance students took Band, Chorus and other electives with the Traditional students, leaving teachers free to hold team meetings. The sixth period had several functions for Renaissance students: seminars, Foreign Language Enrichment Programs (FLEP), independent study programs and physical education were scheduled during this period. The Renpro staff believed that there was a need for reinforcing foreign languages skills when students were not taking a foreign language, so the FLEP was designed to do this. The FLEP was scheduled only for the two trimesters when a student would not be enrolled in a foreign language class. During the trimester when a student was taking a foreign language, this time was used for an independent study program. All of these programs were scheduled on alternate days.

The seventh period was designed as an extra help/planning period and Renaissance students met on alternate days with their first or second morning class teacher. The district had a regular extra help period for all students in the Traditional program in an optional eighth period. In total, Renpro students took 13% more credits than did the Tradpro students, in addition to their seminars, independent study, and FLEP.

There were nine teachers on the Renaissance staff. Math, science, and English were each taught by one teacher who was responsible for two Renpro classes each trimester (or six classes for the year), and for conducting afternoon seminars and advising independent study students. Two social studies teachers each taught one Renpro class and two Tradpro classes, and conducted seminars.

Three foreign languages had to be offered to both Renpro and Tradpro students, and enrollments could not justify full time Renpro teachers for each language. Therefore, two foreign language teachers taught one Renpro class and two traditional classes each day, and conducted the FLEP program. Neither could enrollments justify full time art and computer science Renpro teachers: an art teacher and a computer science teacher each taught one Renpro class and three traditional classes each day, but did not participate in seminars or independent study.

Masconomet had separate honors sections in most subjects: however, after considerable discussion of research concerning grouping, the Renaissance staff proposed that Renpro freshmen identified as honors students be grouped heterogeneously in English and social studies. Separate honors sections were retained in math and science in the Renaissance program, and were offered to students in all courses in the Traditional program.

Since the curriculum was the same for both Renpro and Tradpro students, teachers in both programs agreed to administer the same midyear and final exams.

The 1990-91 Renaissance Program

The second year of the Renaissance Program was changed because of Massachusetts' serious economic problems and the fact that foundation funds were needed to keep the program operating. It should be noted that the cost of operating an entire school under a Copernican schedule would have been no more than operating one under a traditional schedule. However, the cost of operating two, much smaller school programs with similar offerings but incompatible schedules was higher.

The Renaissance classes were increased from 100 minutes to 118 minutes, and Renpro students had 118 hours in class time compared to the Tradpro classes of 139 hours, or about 18% less time. However, in science where Tradpro students had special lab periods, the difference was between 162 hours and 118 hours, a 37% difference. Renpro teachers felt that the longer 118 minute period would be more effective and that it fit nicely with the afternoon schedule which provided extra help for all students.

Sixteen teachers taught in the Renaissance Program in its second year. However, because of financial limitations, all teachers taught one Renpro class each trimester and three Tradpro classes. This required all teachers to teach four classes each day. The FLEP program was continued as an overload for the Renpro foreign language teachers. There were 30 ninth grade and 60 tenth grade students enrolled in the Renaissance program in 1990-91.

The climate was affected by several factors. The Copernican schedule was opposed by some teachers when the plan was first proposed. Some teachers opposed it because they did not believe that the curriculum could be "covered" in significantly fewer hours and that teachers and students would be "burned out" by the intensity of the long classes. Some opposed it for job security reasons: while it was possible to reduce class size by 20% if all teachers taught six rather than five classes each year, it was also possible to leave class sizes at present levels and reduce the staff by 20%. The district had suffered RIF (reductions in force) in the past due to difficult funding problems, which intensified these fears, even though the School Committee had agreed not to RIF tenured teachers while the pilot program was being implemented.

The program got off to a poor start politically. In August, 1989, after budgets were set for the year, there was a reduction in local aid for schools from the Commonwealth. The three towns that comprise the Masconomet district and contribute about 75% of its budget lost an average of 20% of their state aid, and Masconomet lost about 10% of its direct state aid. The towns and schools were forced to cut staff and programs. Renaissance program funding could not be significantly cut because most of it was firmly contracted in teacher salaries. Funding problems intensified concerns about jobs and criticism from town officials that new programs should not be initiated when funds are short.

The heterogeneous grouping of Renaissance honors students in English and social studies for the first year of the program proved to be particularly controversial. It became, in fact, as one opposing parent put it, a "holy war." Many citizens believed that the Renaissance program was the first step in an unannounced plan to eliminate ability grouping. At a School Committee meeting in January, 1990, a large group of parents presented a petition which opposed continuing the Renpro and which was signed by parents of "75% of the members of the National Honor Society." The School Committee voted 8 to 3 to continue the program in 1990-91, but considerably limited its FY91 funding.

In March, 1990, the School District lost its Proposition 2 1/2 override elections and had to reduce its budget, including cutting financial support for the Renpro to $20,000. It authorized the superintendent to seek outside funds, which had to be in place by the end of May. Surprisingly, the money was raised just in time, including $83,000 in two grants and about $25,000 raised by the Renpro parents. But political problems continued despite favorable interim reports evaluating the Renpro. Two School Committee members who strongly supported the Renpro lost their seats to candidates who opposed the program, reducing support to a 6 to 5 majority.

During the first year, several hundred visitors came from all parts of the country to examine the program, and the media coverage was substantial. National interest and the favorable interim report from the evaluation did not unify the staffs. There was a great deal of criticism centered on the allegation that the program "divided" the ninth grade class.

The School Committee decided in September, 1990 to terminate the Renaissance program at the end of the academic year. Reasons varied from teacher association opposition to the divisions within the school, to the concern that a divided school community might have an adverse impact on passing Proposition 2 1/2 overrides, to the fear that the district would have to RIF teachers.

Many positive elements came out of the experience: Renpro teachers, students and their parents were very supportive of the program throughout its duration, though they were only a minority of the total community. The favorable evaluations, the fact that more teachers wanted to join the Renaissance program, and national recognition received by the program were very positive outcomes.

THE EVALUATION

Overview

This report provides the results of our evaluation of the Renaissance program as implemented at the Masconomet Regional High School for the two years 1989-90 and 1990-91. The data are presented for each year separately. The first year (1989-90) and the second year (1990-91) were both years of implementation, and follow-up assessments were made in the fall of 1991, after the Renaissance students had returned to the Traditional program.

This evaluation includes data from participants (students, parents, teachers and administrators) in both the Renaissance and Traditional programs. Over the course of the 1989-90 academic year, we conducted some 65 hours of classroom observations; interviews with school counselors, department chairs, and teachers in both programs; surveys of students, teachers, and parents in both programs; telephone interviews with both Renaissance and Traditional parents; group interviews with both Renaissance and Traditional students; follow-up interviews with Renaissance teachers; and statistical analyses of student academic performance on midterm and final examinations.

During the 1990-1991 academic year, we conducted interviews with students (and their parents) who transferred from the Renaissance back into the Traditional Program after one year, and surveyed teachers' opinions of the program. We continued our evaluation of academic achievement by conducting tests (1) to assess students' levels of retention of course material at three points during the year, and (2) to assess performance in the second year. In the fall of 1991, we interviewed those students who had been in the Renaissance program for both years of its existence, and were now back in the Traditional program. We also evaluated domain understanding, group collaboration skills, and thinking dispositions for both former Renaissance students and Traditional students.

THE FIRST YEAR (1989-1990)

Surveys and Interviews

November, 1989: Counselor Interviews: The evaluation began with interviews of the school counselors. During the fall of the first year, the Masconomet school counselors had spoken informally with many of the students in the Renaissance Program. They told us that students in the Renaissance program were enjoying their school experiences: they were very satisfied with longer periods and small classes, and with the fact that they only had to concentrate on two courses at once. Students also felt that the teachers knew them better and more personally than did their teachers the previous year.

Three negative aspects of the program were also reported to the counselors by the students. First, students missed seeing their friends in the Traditional program. Second, they found the seminar period somewhat disorganized. Third, they were unhappy with the extra help time.

November, 1989: Department Chair Interviews: The interviews with the department chairs, also conducted in the fall of 1989, revealed both positive and negative aspects of the Renaissance program. All spoke positively about the small classes, the time allotted to each subject, and the quick turnaround on graded work. They were pleased that the teachers were better able to know the students on a personal level, and that there was a high degree of student involvement and student-teacher interaction. They also mentioned how well the teachers were prepared.

The department chairs, however, expressed the concern that teachers were finding the Renaissance program demanding. They were concerned over whether teachers could cover the material in the allotted time, whether the students would retain the information which was presented to them so quickly, and whether material covered so rapidly might negatively affect the quality of the students' work. Teachers had to struggle too with how to manage the varying academic needs of the Honors and regular students. They expressed concern that if the Renaissance program expanded and class size were increased, the number of teaching jobs at the school might be reduced. Finally, because of the demands on teachers, the department chairs felt that it would be preferable if a teacher taught in either the Renaissance or the Traditional program, but not in both.

December, 1989: Student Questionnaires: A questionnaire was designed to elicit students' perceptions of their programs. It tapped issues such as teaching styles, classroom activities, and perceptions of teachers (see Appendix A). Analyses showed that Renpro students, in contrast to students in the Traditional program, felt that their teachers more frequently individualized course work to meet their academic needs, cared more about them, and knew them better. Renpro students reported a significantly higher frequency of student-teacher dialogue, both about schoolwork and other issues.

Students in the Renaissance program reported that they were more comfortable speaking out and voicing their opinions in class, and they worked in small groups more frequently, had more class discussions, and were more satisfied with the length of their classes than were the Traditional program students. Overall, Renaissance program students indicated a higher level of satisfaction with their program than did the Traditional program students. A larger percentage of students in the Renaissance program indicated that they participated in the decision to be in the program.

Some trends were also apparent, although they were not as pronounced as the differences mentioned above. Specifically, the Renaissance program students were more satisfied with the amount of material covered in class, thought that the subjects taught in school were more interesting, and felt that they knew their classmates better. However, they did not enjoy their seminar or FLEP periods, nor were they satisfied with their learning experiences in the seminar period.

Tradpro students, to a higher degree than Renpro students, felt that they understood the material being taught, and that it was useful to them in daily life.

May, 1990: Student Interviews: In the spring of the first Renaissance year, groups of students in both programs were interviewed to probe those aspects of the school experience which the questionnaire administered the previous fall had indicated were significant to them. The topics covered included strengths of the program, concerns, relationships with teachers and classmates, relevance of academic studies to daily life, homework assignments, and extra-curricular activities.

The Renaissance students saw the academic structure of the program as a strength. They stated that it was easier to concentrate on two courses, which resulted in deeper understanding and higher grades. They enjoyed starting new courses every twelve weeks "because it doesn't get boring" and they "learn so much more." In general, they described the program as relaxed and "easy going." They felt that the program fostered close relationships with teachers, relative to the previous year, and they felt better able to discuss issues among themselves and to work out problems. They felt that their learning was also enhanced as a result of increased rapport with their teachers and their classmates: "It just seems like a family." Academically, they felt challenged to perform at a higher level, and this benefitted their learning experience.

Concerns of the Renaissance students included feeling under pressure to perform well. Those taking foreign languages were concerned about how much they would retain. Some felt that they were not learning as much because "it seemed so much easier," but others suggested that it was difficult to catch up if they fell behind.

Renaissance students were bothered that some Traditional students felt they were not required to do much work, especially in Honors courses. As a result, Renaissance students felt that there was "too much pressure to do well." Some expressed the feeling that "if anything goes wrong, the Renaissance program gets blamed." For example, "the sports fees are going up next year and they blame the Renaissance program."

There was a general consensus that the teachers and students in the Renaissance program were more involved in school, due to their closer personal relationships. Personal relationships were facilitated by smaller, fewer and longer classes; they permitted teachers to "have a lot more time to individualize," "some teachers get really personal, which is 'cool'," and "it's nice that we can see the teachers outside of the classroom setting, like in the Renpro room." One student stated that he was getting better grades "because I usually don't get along with my teachers, but this year, it's different since I have time to get to know them." English was selected by more Renaissance students as the subject that was most relevant to their daily life.

Renaissance students felt that homework was easy and that there was sufficient time to finish it in class or during the extra help period time. Their homework was easy because they did not have to do as much "busy work." The work assigned was more meaningful and tied in to the next day's lesson. It taught them to take more responsibility for finishing their work daily: "if you don't do it, you fall behind fast."

When asked about the seminar program, Renaissance students regarded it as similar to a study hall. The activities mentioned repeatedly were "sitting around, and talking about something." The seminar had little structure or agenda. Students were, however, aware of the fact that the teachers had invested effort in the seminar program.

In the interviews, the Traditional students were asked the same questions as the Renaissance students, with the exception of questions about the seminar program. The strengths that the Traditional students mentioned were the Honors program (which consisted of separate Honors sections for each course), class length, and the general structure of their program. There was a consensus that the Honors program was intellectually stimulating, well-taught, and a very important element of the Traditional program. Students enjoyed having all their classes for the entire length of the year, because "it's more like college," "you don't get bored with your worst subjects," and "you can start something fresh every forty-five minutes." Some general comments made about the strengths of the Traditional program were "we're used to this, we've accepted it — the workload and stuff," "there are more electives to choose from," and "it's easier to keep up."

Dividing the school into two programs seemed to be a significant factor in the school experience of the Traditional students. Some felt competition with the Renaissance students and were concerned about needing to perform well on examinations.

The Traditional students perceived the grading for the Renaissance students to be easier, and the work to be less structured. They viewed the Renaissance program negatively, and resented it when students did better academically in the Renaissance program. Traditional students did not feel particularly close to each other but, in general, expressed considerable satisfaction with their teachers and classmates. They saw a clearer distinction between the roles of teachers and students. They did express dissatisfaction with the lack of interaction with their Renaissance classmates.

The Traditional students spoke about the relevance of their academic studies this year to their daily life because "you deal with English every day, like even to read a newspaper." The students gave examples from their science and math classes, stating that the teachers made an effort to show them how the subject they were studying was relevant.

The time spent on homework by the Traditional students varied from approximately thirty minutes to two hours; however, they were able to complete most of their daily homework in study hall. Some formed study groups because "you don't feel like you're working when you do it in groups," and "talking about it, like when you have to explain something to someone else, helps me understand it."

June, 1990: Student Interviews: In June, 1990, we surveyed students on several aspects of achievement motivation (see Appendix B). Research literature has suggested that students' academic achievement is enhanced by (1) beliefs that effort is more important than ability in determining school performance, (2) beliefs that both one's effort and ability are not limited, and (3) parental involvement in students' education (Weiner, Russell & Lerman, 1972; Dweck & Bempechat, 1983; Nicholls, 1984; Jagacinski & Nicholls, 1987). When we examined students' attributions for success and failure in math, the results were somewhat contradictory. For example, there was a tendency for Renaissance students to believe more strongly than Traditional students that natural ability and ease of course work were important factors in doing well in school. However, when asked about failure, the Traditional students felt significantly more strongly than Renaissance students that lack of ability was the important factor.

In both programs, when students' attributions for success and failure were correlated with their grades, high grades were associated with the belief that success was due to effort. Traditional students, however, were significantly more likely than Renaissance students to believe that intelligence is unlimited. Relative to Traditional students, Renaissance students believed significantly more often that it is important to know math to get a good job, and they looked forward to taking more math classes.

Finally, the results showed no differences between Renaissance and Traditional students in their perceptions of their parents' interest in their education when they were in elementary school. However, as teenagers, the Traditional students reported significantly more parental involvement than Renaissance students. For example, they perceived that there was parental sacrifice for their education and parental control over such matters as holding a part-time job.

October, 1989: Classroom Observations. December, 1989: Teacher Survey. May, 1990: Teacher Interviews. Classroom observations revealed that Renaissance teachers engaged their classes in more group work, cooperative learning, and individualized instruction than Traditional teachers. Both the smaller classes and the extended class periods encouraged these activities.

Teachers in the Renaissance Program were very enthusiastic about the new program, particularly with the way it challenged them to examine their teaching strategies and allowed them to get to know their students (see Appendix C). Teachers felt revitalized by the interactions with their colleagues and their discussions about teaching. They did have concerns about teaching the seminar, pressure to cover material, and the reservations of some colleagues who were not involved in the Renaissance program. "Allpro" teachers, who taught in both programs, had similar perceptions. They also found their schedules too demanding and had little preparation time. Some felt socially isolated because they were unable to participate regularly in the Renaissance teachers meetings.

Teachers in the Renaissance program had excellent personal relationships with their students and saw this as a measure of their success. They took advantage of the smaller classes and longer periods which allowed for more individualized relationships. They described their close associations as the highlight of their teaching. Renaissance teachers also individualized instruction more than they had in the past. They felt that they knew the strengths and weaknesses of each student, and that the smaller classes encouraged students' active participation in discussions. Like their students, teachers felt that their interactions were on a very personal level. Classroom observations confirmed these reports.

Teachers felt renewed enthusiasm for their profession. The longer class periods forced them to examine their teaching practices, and to do innovative planning. The longer classes allowed more time for students to tie ideas together and make deeper connections. Teachers shared in these accomplishments, in spite of their concerns about being able to cover the proscribed material. In the classrooms, Renaissance teachers used group activities twice as often as Traditional teachers. Certainly teaching in the Renaissance program challenged teachers to redesign their teaching strategies. Looking back, they felt that the 45 minute period was extremely inefficient.

Teachers and students alike were pleased with the quick turnaround on students' papers. They were able to go over student work while it was still fresh in everybody's mind. This increased students' intensity and depth of coverage. Teachers also discovered that students were able to do much more on their own than they had assumed: they wondered how much more improvement there could be. A few teachers reported that students expected to do less work in the Renaissance program, and that they were terribly surprised to find it required more.

In the spring, Renaissance teachers became more concerned about the lack of time. Many found their schedule physically and mentally demanding. Some could not find the right approach to teaching the seminar. Others were troubled about the Renpro-Tradpro division. Art teachers were concerned about the lack of time for reflection. Finally, some teachers were troubled by students' having a subject for one trimester, and then not again until the final trimester of the following year.

As mentioned earlier, Allpro teachers again found that working in both programs was particularly demanding; shifting programs required shifting gears with no break during the day. The Renaissance teachers, however, continually highlighted the positive aspects of this program, and in our final interviews, the tone continued to be one of praise. All of the teachers hoped the program would continue and wished to teach in the Renaissance program for its second year.

The shorter modules had mixed results. The independent study period and the seminar were both frustrating to teachers. The independent study was disappointing because students were not committed to the task. Teachers themselves felt unprepared to conduct the seminars. They lost seminar time due to testing and other events. The FLEP program, however, was extremely beneficial. Teaching an entire course each trimester allowed teachers to push their teaching further.

At mid-year, teachers spoke about the high quality of their relationships with students, attributing it to the "luxury of smaller classes." In our final interviews, the theme of excellent rapport was again reiterated, with additional comments from teachers about "how nicely cohesive the kids have become with each other." Finally, Renaissance teachers felt that during the second year they would want to "tighten ship" by having all students take responsibility for their learning.

As the year progressed, Renaissance teachers became increasingly frustrated by being confined to the curriculum. The way that the Renaissance program was to be evaluated was partly responsible for the restrictions: teachers had agreed to teach the same curriculum in both programs so that student performance could be compared. Renaissance teachers felt they could have made their classes more productive if they could have gone into more depth in their subjects, although this approach might have resulted in less breadth of material. Trying to teach parallel curricula inhibited the Renaissance program's potential to build on the concentrated learning time. Teachers found that work in the Renaissance program was conceptually different, specifically mentioning that multiple choice exams were a poor indicator of achievement.

There was a continuing concern about the Honors program in the Renaissance program, which consisted of separate Honors sections for math and science, and heterogeneous grouping for Honors students in the other courses. There seemed to be no clear distinction for the Honors students, nor a clear definition of Honors work in the Renaissance program. Teachers felt that their students had done high quality work, but decisions about the "extra" work for Honors students were a bit of a problem.

When discussing the support they received, teachers found their work with an invited consultant who suggested new pedagogical approaches for their use of the seminars most beneficial. They expressed a desire for more training in cooperative learning. Teachers felt they had the support of the administration, though some felt that the second year's scheduling should be better, as at times there was an overlap in department meetings and Renaissance meetings.

Renaissance teachers were surprised by the number of visitors to the school, but enjoyed describing their activities and felt that it did no harm to students' learning. They were still concerned about the lack of communication between the two programs. They expressed a desire to improve the dialogue and the amount of time they could spend with the teachers in the Traditional program. Nevertheless, the tension observed at mid-year seemed much decreased.

For the Renaissance teachers, the first year of the program was successful. From the first challenges of scheduling, teachers continually reflected on their practice. They re-examined their teaching, and saw their students anew. Though tired, they spoke highly of the program and the excellence of the first year. The teachers were eager to continue with the program.

The Fall survey and Spring interviews revealed that Traditional teachers did not find the first year easy. They perceived that the Renaissance program called their teaching capabilities into question. They felt that they had to justify their successful program. Because much attention was given to the Renaissance program, they felt isolated and constrained by comparisons between the Traditional and Renaissance programs.

Some Traditional teachers were concerned that the atmosphere of the Renaissance program gave more freedom to students. In year-end interviews, Traditional teachers expressed the feeling that the whole ninth grade curriculum was better now and that teachers had been empowered this year. As one teacher stated, "[the fact] that kids love school is a great accomplishment." Another Traditional teacher said "I think teachers from the Renaissance Program should receive great kudos for what they developed."

December, 1989: Parent Questionnaire: Our earliest questionnaire to parents revealed that they felt that information about the Renaissance program and implications regarding the future education of their children was communicated well, and that they were satisfied with the communications from the school administration (see Appendix D). Most of the Renaissance parents supported the enrollment of their children in the Renaissance program, because they observed such marked improvements in their children's attitudes toward school. Teachers knew their children better, and they liked the smaller classes.

Renaissance parents were disappointed with the seminar, independent study, and extra help periods. They felt, however, that their children had been motivated by the Renaissance program, were more enthusiastic about school, and were obtaining better grades. They would have liked to have been notified more often about their child's progress.

The Traditional parents believed that the better teachers taught in the Renaissance program, that Traditional classes were too large, and that Renaissance students received less homework. They indicated that there was some family concern over deciding in which program to enroll their children. They also worried more about the school district's budget.

May, 1990: Parent Telephone Interviews: Telephone interviews were conducted with randomly selected parents (see Appendix E). Renaissance parents viewed the trimester structure, class size and length, teacher and student relationships, and homework assignments as strengths of the program. Their children enjoyed "getting into" a subject, ideal for building motivation "because six or seven subjects a day can be overwhelming." Renaissance parents observed that their children participated in and enjoyed more group work and discussions. The longer class length "turned out to be no problem," although a few parents commented that their child's attention span seemed shorter than that. The longer period of time encouraged teachers to individualize their teaching, and enabled the student to obtain "continuity, exploration, and in-depth instruction."

There was general consensus among Renaissance parents that there was an improvement in their child's relationships with his or her teachers. "The kids work harder because they're being closely observed and the child understands the teachers' expectations." The parent-teacher relationship improved as well, because "there is an opportunity to talk to the teacher more often."

All comments about homework were positive. "Homework in the past was like pulling teeth, but now it's enjoyable. Before, three-quarters of it was not done." "She's doing much more homework, but thinks it's less because she doesn't consider reading to be homework." Parents were concerned with retention, the pace and scheduling of classes, and tension about the program.

Retention concerns focused on math and foreign languages: "how long is it going to take to get back into the swing of the subject?" One perspective was, "maybe they will retain more because of the happy and relaxed atmosphere." The seminar program was perceived as dysfunctional and many students did not know how to participate in a discussion. Tension about the division in the school caused by the existence of two programs was a problem. Many were concerned about the future of the program. Some stated that their child would be "heartbroken if it doesn't continue." Parents felt that the program met their educational aspirations for their children, based on the high caliber of teachers, the improvement in their child's attitude toward school, and the flexibility of scheduling.

Parents' overall experience of their child's enrollment in the Renaissance program the first year was very good. Most seemed pleased with the growth in learning: "the time and energy of the program has enabled her to capture thought processes," "to listen to others," " to have a positive attitude toward learning," and "to have time for creative thoughts." They were also impressed with the teachers whom they described as being "very involved, and their enthusiasm has spread to the kids." Some concrete ratings of the program included "I give it an A," and "on a scale of one to ten, I give it a nine."

The Traditional parents saw the Honors program, the curriculum, and the teaching to be the highlights of their child's program. The Honors program prepared students well for college and provided a supportive atmosphere for the studious. The parents liked courses being taught throughout the year which allowed for "more depth" because of continuity. The Traditional program encouraged "well-rounded student development" and the teachers were of high quality. Many parents felt that the

Traditional program encouraged a sense of personal responsibility towards learning. These parents were concerned about the division of the ninth grade and felt that class size in the Traditional program had grown as a result of the Renaissance program.

The parents were extremely satisfied with their child's experience in the Traditional program. Nothing educational was lacking, and there was an overall consensus of high standards. They reported a positive attitude toward school and learning in their children.

Academic Performance

The academic performance of each program was analyzed by comparing the midterm exams of each Renaissance trimester with the midyear exams of the Traditional students, and the final exams of each trimester with the Traditional end-of-year exams. Teachers in both programs used the same curriculum, and the same midterm and final exams were administered to students. To make valid comparisons between these two groups of students, their academic strengths as they began their respective ninth grade programs were compared. Students' scores on the eighth grade Iowa Test of Basic Skills indicated that the Traditional students had significantly higher reading scores than did the Renaissance students. The Traditional students also scored higher in mathematics, but not significantly so. Using the statistical method of analysis of covariance, reading ability was held constant in all the analyses that follow.

Midterm Examinations

Renaissance students scored significantly higher than Traditional students on the English-Essay midyear exams, while the Traditional students scored significantly higher on the English-Multiple Choice exam (see Table 1). The differences between the groups offset each other, and disappeared when English total scores were compared. Questions were raised about teachers scoring their own students' essay exams. Therefore, an independent reader re-scored all essay exams for both groups. Analysis of the re-scored essays confirmed that the Renaissance students performed significantly higher than did the Traditional students. These essays were a more authentic measure of students' achievements than were the multiple choice tests' results, so this finding was especially significant.

Renaissance students scored significantly higher than Traditional students in Spanish, while Traditional students outperformed Renaissance students in Science Honors.

There was a tendency favoring the Renaissance students in Social Studies and Algebra I, and there was a tendency favoring the Traditional students in Science, but these were not statistically significant.

No differences were found for French, German, English-Total, Algebra 1A or Geometry.

Final Examinations

On end-of-year examinations (see Table 2), Renaissance students scored significantly higher on English-M and Science-H. Traditional students scored significantly higher on Algebra, and tended to score higher on Geometry. There were no differences between the groups on English-E, English-T, Algebra 1A, Social Studies, Science, or any of the language courses, although the Renaissance students tended to score higher in Spanish.

Summary

In sum, the first year's data showed that there was no subject in which students of one program consistently performed better than students of the other. In most subjects, there were no differences between the groups, indicating that students in both programs were performing at similar levels, despite differences in the structure of the programs and in time spent on task. The Renaissance program did achieve its academic objectives in its first year.

THE SECOND YEAR (1990-1991)

The second year evaluation focused on four areas:

1. interviews with students who left the Renaissance program, and with their parents,

2 interviews with Renaissance students who were in the program for both years,

3. a survey of teacher opinions,

4. the academic performance of students in both programs.

Evaluation of academic performance included periodic tests of retention of material covered in the first year (Gap tests) and tests of achievement in the second year.

Surveys and Interviews

September, 1990: Interviews with Students Who Left the Renaissance Program: At the beginning of the 1990-91 school year, twenty-six former Renaissance students switched into the Traditional program. Students who did so were interviewed.

Most of the students had mixed views of Renaissance. They liked certain aspects of the program, but were dissatisfied with others. Often, the major cause of dissatisfaction was a by-product of scheduling. Specifically, the social implications of being in a program separated from the rest of the school seemed to play a major role in students' decisions to leave the program. Students found that smaller classes, coupled with fewer opportunities to move throughout the school, tended to decrease student interaction.

Interaction was further reduced by the structure of the Renaissance program. In the first year, the Renaissance students were physically separated from the rest of the school population because the classes of the two programs began and ended at different times. Several complained of relationships severed by the divisions as "some kids didn't get to see other kids when they were split apart." Some students reported that they were unhappy enough with the social implications of being in Renaissance that they abandoned it for that reason alone. Others also regretted losing the academic aspect of Renaissance, but social demands took precedence in the mind of many students. "In the regular (Traditional classes) you don't really learn that much. So, in a way it's kind of bad that I switched because I wanted to be in the regular system." Some students reported intense parental opposition to switching back to the Traditional program: "My parents like Renpro, only because I did better. They just, they assume since my grades went up that I did a lot better in it, and it was because of the program, which was unfair. I only had to take two classes, and if I only had to take two classes in Traditional I would probably do the same thing." Another student, however, reported that his/her parent forced the switch out of the Renaissance program because the parent wanted the child to have math every day.

There was no pattern regarding the amount or difficulty of homework. About one third of the students said they had had more homework in Renaissance, another third reported more work in the Traditional program, and the remainder saw no difference. Students revealed that the homework assignments were more important for success in the Renaissance program: "(in Traditional) it's very easy to let yourself slack off, but you can't in Renpro." "You had to do your homework to know what's going on in Renpro. In Traditional, you do it just to do it." "The work (in Renpro) was a lot harder. You could never get out of doing anything, so I guess you learned more."

Two students expressed dissatisfaction with the program because they were not able to have a favorite subject in their schedule on a daily basis. "Personally, I value art a lot," one student reported, saying that he/she was unhappy during the 120 days that his/her schedule did not contain an art class. "Last year (in Renpro), I had photography, and I took art as a block, and we didn't get to do as many projects as the Traditional kids do because we didn't have the time."

Most students who talked about individual subjects in Renpro liked English and social studies. Math was the most controversial subject. Several students, however, found advantages in Renpro math instruction: "Like in geometry, I need help, and I can't, like, ask for help in the middle of class like you could in Renpro." Students seemed to value the pedagogic changes in math instruction in Renpro classes (classes provided structured, small group collaborative learning, and one-on-one help during the latter half of the time period), as well as the smaller classes created by the nature of the Renpro program.

Another student preferred math in a traditional format, but thought other subjects were well suited for Renpro: "I would like to have geometry in Traditional, but I liked having Western Civ (in Renpro) because it was more like telling a story and everything and I liked having that, and I liked having English, because you could discuss things."

Most students reported that relationships were better with teachers in Renaissance. Typical comments included: "They get to know you better. You aren't just a number. They learn your name by the second day of class. They were, like, friends. They were people."

Some Honors students who switched from the Renaissance program to the Traditional program complained about the awarding of grades and honors credit in Renpro. "I want to get into a good college. It will be harder because Renpro kids have an advantage in computing class rank." "They (Renpro students) got honors credit when they didn't deserve it." Some Tradpro students complained that the Renpro kids never seemed to go home with any books.

Many students had given considerable thought to what the school system should do with the Renaissance program, and had specific recommendations. One Honors student, who felt overburdened when he was scheduled into math and science during the same trimester, thought that Renaissance was preferable, but that scheduling should be arranged so that math and science, or English and social studies, were not scheduled in the same trimester. Another student, who found the 100 minute periods too long, thought that a good compromise would be to schedule three classes to run for a semester. Many students wished that they could take certain classes in Renpro format, others in Traditional mode.

December/January 1990/91: Parent Interviews: Sixteen of the families whose children had switched out of Renpro were contacted.[1] Fifteen open-ended interviews were conducted[2] around impressions of the program, whether it met expectations, homework, grades, courses, curriculum, attitude towards school, reasons for the decision to change programs, parents' view of the change, and their opinion of the decision. Interviews generally lasted about one hour.

Most parents held strong views about the Renaissance program. Opinions ranged from strong support to vehement opposition. No parent reported having observed a Renpro class. Half of the parents were overwhelmingly positive ("Wonderful, very innovative, kids had to get involved in their learning as a result of program's design, everything education is supposed to be."). Four parents were positive about the program, but did not feel that it had been right for their child ("Pleased with the program, but it didn't work for my child. Wonderful concept."). Two parents expressed negative overall views ("Too open, too much free time, not structured. When my child returned to the Traditional program, he had trouble adjusting.").

Six parents were overwhelmingly positive in their view that the program had met expectations ("Absolutely. My child was excited and involved."). Four parents were quite negative ("No. The district did not follow through on promises of additional help that resulted from smaller classes."). The remaining parents held mixed views. One parent saw the program as an essentially good one, but perhaps not suited for all students. Two others raised their concerns about the issue of retention.

Parents were asked about homework in the two programs. Six parents saw no difference between homework in the programs. Four parents believed that more homework was assigned in the Renaissance program, while three believed more work was assigned in the Traditional program. One parent did state that students had the time in class to complete homework under the supervision of the teacher, which was an advantage for the Renaissance program.

Parents were asked to comment on differences in student grades that could be attributed to the Renaissance program. Seven parents noticed a dramatic improvement in their children's grades, while seven others noted no difference at all. One

---

[1] The parents were called between 5:00 p.m. and 9:00 p.m. Messages were not left on answering machines, and the first parent to answer the phone was asked to participate in the survey.

[2] One parent was not sure in which program their child was enrolled, and had no concept of what the Renaissance program was.

parent recorded a decrease in performance from the previous year. Some parents attributed the grade improvement to the structure of the program (i.e., having only two subjects at once, and thus not feeling overwhelmed).

Parents were asked if they noticed any difference in the Renaissance program across course subjects, or if any subjects were better suited for one or the other program. While students often mentioned that they preferred math in the Renpro format, parents did not voice that opinion. Parents were more likely to praise Renpro for social studies and English, and to dislike instruction in other subjects ("Math was not as good, too much material to digest in too little time." " My child enjoyed Mr. A in English. The program gave more time to study plays and literature in depth.").

Parents were asked if there was a difference in the curriculum between groups. Most parents did not notice a large difference. Those who noticed a difference thought that more critical thinking and discussion skills were fostered by the Renpro program ("Tradpro emphasizes more memorization and rote learning, more critical thinking skills in Renpro."). One was actually disappointed that there was not more of a difference: "We wanted to see extra projects and more in-depth work for Honors students."

Parents were asked if they noticed a change in attitude toward school. Generally, parents seemed to view their students as having a better attitude toward academics, but were unhappy about the social isolation of the program ("At the end, my child felt socially isolated in Renpro as result of the division of the school." "My child developed wonderful relationships with teachers and sits in on a class with a former Renpro teacher as a result of the relationship." "My child is really involved and active in learning.") .

Parents were asked why their child changed programs. Two parents said that the decision had been theirs ("I felt the year was a waste." "I thought my child was getting more challenging work in Traditional, and I didn't want to risk lower SAT scores by having my child in an experimental program."). Reasons cited by other parents included their child's feelings of social isolation and concerns about college preparation, and the boredom that resulted from longer class periods.

Parents were asked if they supported their child's decision to move to Tradpro (when it had been the child's choice). Most were supportive of their children's decision ("I wanted to see my child stay in Renpro, but I approved because my child's wishes were precipitated by social factors.").

When asked, most parents believed that the Renaissance program should remain in some form. Most thought it should be incorporated into the school on a limited basis. For example: "I hate to see it finished. I would like to see a follow-up, incorporating successful elements of Renpro into the regular school day. I would want to see one class for all students, that is, I would not want to see students segregated by program."

"I still support Renpro, but I worry about its impact on cost and college admission."

"The district should not eliminate Renpro, nor should it convert the school to Renpro, but should offer choice, unless prohibitively expensive."

Focus Group

A group of freshmen was presented with an overview of the research findings for comment. They agreed that most of the findings were consistent with their attitudes and those of their classmates. The group, however, disagreed with several findings, and offered several views that were not previously recorded. They disagreed with the findings that the program was divisive: "We were in different teams in junior high, now we're in different programs. What's the difference?" "My friends didn't change just because they were in (a different program)."

Students attributed the controversy and divisiveness more to adults, and were somewhat critical of parents, junior high teachers, and school committee members. Freshmen complained that the most vocal parents and school committee members did not have adequate knowledge of what was happening at Masconomet: "These parents never came to see what was happening here." "I've never seen a parent in one of my classes."

Those focus group members who expressed an interest in having the option of Renpro classes were not in consensus about which classes they would select. Students were most likely to want Renpro classes in math, science, and English, and least likely to want elective courses (except computer science) in the Renpro format. Students were evenly split when asked if they would like foreign language in Renpro, and were firm in their arguments on both sides of the question.

In most cases, students across all groups (class, program, gender) were essentially in favor of student choice. Ultimately, they asked "Why couldn't they leave us alone and let us have both programs?"

June, 1991: Teacher Survey: A total of 44 teachers (29 Traditional, 15 Renaissance) responded to a survey that was placed in their mailboxes at the school (see Appendix F). The survey sought teachers' opinions on the quality of teaching and learning, their relationships with students, and the political aspects of carrying two programs at the school.

Not surprisingly, teachers' opinions tended to support the program of which they were a part. Several significant differences in opinion between the Traditional and Renaissance teachers emerged. Renaissance teachers believed more than Traditional teachers that Renaissance students should be allowed to continue their schooling in the Renaissance format, that double periods are conducive to quality education, that the two-course format encourages students to gain more depth of understanding, and that the program improved students' attitudes towards learning. Renaissance teachers believed that math could be successfully taught in their program, felt that the lecture format of instruction was too prevalent at the school, and that incorporating the strengths of the Renaissance program into the curriculum could improve the quality of education. They believed more strongly than Traditional teachers that getting to know students better should be a goal of teaching and that the Renaissance format is more conducive than the Traditional to the development of student/teacher rapport. Finally, Renaissance teachers indicated a preference for teaching a new course each year, while Tradpro teachers were quite neutral on these points.

In contrast, Traditional teachers believed more strongly that 45 minute periods are conducive to quality education, that the Renaissance teachers lowered their standards and inflated their grades, that Renaissance classes were less rigorous than Traditional classes, and that the Renaissance program posed a threat to the school's Honors program. Traditional teachers felt less valued at the school.

In answer to questions about the political climate at the school, Traditional teachers felt more strongly that it might take a long time to heal the divisions caused by the Renaissance program. Renaissance teachers felt more strongly that political considerations led to the demise of the program, that the school should offer both programs, and that it would be better to have an all-Renaissance school than an all-Traditional school. Finally, if given the choice of both programs, Renaissance teachers were more encouraging than Traditional teachers for their children to enroll in the Renaissance program.

ACADEMIC PERFORMANCE

Gap Testing

During the second year, in September, December and March, comparisons were made of the retention of material studied during the first year. These comparisons, referred to as "Gap tests," were administered from 3 months to 15 months after the courses ended. In September, exams were given to all tenth grade students who had participated in the first year: depending on when first-year courses ended, gaps from final exams to the September testing ranged from 3 months to 9 months. To reduce the amount of testing, students were then divided randomly into two groups, and were tested again either in December or in March. Gaps for the December exams ranged from 6 months to 12 months, and for the March exams, from 9 months to 15 months.

As mentioned above, students' eighth grade scores on the Iowa Test of Basic Skills indicated that the Traditional students had significantly higher reading ability than the Renaissance students. Statistical methods that held reading ability constant were used to analyze the Gap test results.

Gap tests were administered for the following subjects: English, Algebra 1A, Algebra 1, Geometry, Physical Sciences, and Social Studies. Comparisons of performance between the groups at the three testing points revealed significant differences in retention levels for all subjects with the exception of Algebra 1A (see Tables 3-8).

Renaissance students who had English in the first trimester of ninth grade had a significantly smaller mean difference between their final exams and their Gap tests in March of the second year, indicating that they had retained more material relative to their final exam scores than the Traditional students. Otherwise, there were no differences in retention levels over time for English.

Renaissance students who took Algebra 1 during the third trimester of ninth grade also had a smaller mean difference between their final exams and their Gap tests in March of the second year. For two reasons, this result should be interpreted with caution: the sample size was extremely small in the March group, and this group scored significantly lower than any other group on their final exams so that there may have simply been "less material to lose."

In Geometry, while there were no significant differences between Renaissance and Traditional students in final exam scores or in the September and March Gap tests, the Renaissance students who took Geometry in the second trimester of ninth grade had a significantly larger mean difference between their final exams and the December Gap tests. Renaissance students who took Physical Sciences during the second trimester scored significantly lower on their final exams than the Traditional students. In addition, Renaissance students who took the course during the first trimester had a much larger mean difference between final exam scores and Gap test scores in December than the Traditional students, indicating that they did not retain as much material over time since their final exam scores were comparable.

Renaissance students who took Social Studies in the first and second trimesters had significantly larger mean differences between final exam scores and Gap tests administered in September than the Traditional students.

Summary

Even when one takes into account that Gap test results were compared without regard to the time lapse between final exam and Gap test (which should favor the Traditional program), there were no consistent significant differences that favored students in one program over students in the other. This suggests that, overall, Renaissance and Traditional students retained material at comparable levels.

Ninth Grade Midterm Examinations

There were no significant differences between Renaissance and Traditional students in English, Algebra 1A, Western Civilization, or Physical Sciences. In Algebra 1, second trimester Renaissance students scored significantly higher than their Traditional peers (see Table 9).

Final Examinations

Renaissance students performed significantly better than their Traditional peers in English and Algebra (see Table 10). In Physical Sciences, the Traditional students scored higher than their Renaissance peers who had taken the course in the second trimester, but there was no difference in performance relative to the third trimester Renpro students. There were no significant differences between the groups in Algebra 1A and Western Civilization (see Table 11).

Summary

Renaissance students in the ninth grade during the second year of the program performed significantly better than Traditional students in Algebra on both their midterms and their finals. There were no other consistent significant differences between the two programs, indicating that student performance was similar in both.

Tenth Grade Midterm Examinations

In English, Traditional students scored significantly higher than all Renaissance students. No significant differences emerged between the groups in English Honors, Algebra 1B, Geometry, History, History Honors, Biology or Chemistry (see Table 11).

Final Examinations

All three Renpro groups scored lower than the Traditional group in English, although this difference was significant only for the third trimester comparison. In English Honors, the students in both Renaissance classes scored significantly lower than the Traditional students. In mathematics, there were no significant differences between the groups in Algebra 1B, Geometry, or Trigonometry (see Table 12).

In History, two of the three Renaissance groups scored significantly lower than the Traditional group. The third scored higher than the Traditional group, but this difference was not statistically significant. In History Honors, there were no significant differences between the students in both groups.

There were no differences between groups in Chemistry Honors, even though the Traditional students had 162 classroom hours, while the Renaissance students met for only 118 hours. In Biology, one Renaissance group scored significantly higher than the Traditional group.

Summary

Traditional students in the tenth grade performed better on their midterms and finals than Renaissance students in English and English Honors: most comparisons were statistically significant. In other subjects, differences between programs were inconsistent, indicating that performance in one program was similar to that in the other.

Follow-up Interviews And Assessments (Fall, 1991)

October, 1991: Student Interviews: Seventeen former Renaissance students who had been in the program for the two years of its existence were interviewed in order to probe students' perceptions of their educational experiences. The students were fairly uniform in their comments about their return to the Traditional program. Most discussed the problem of adjustment to taking five major subjects simultaneously, the decline in their grades, the lack of help available from teachers, larger class sizes, and generally feeling disenfranchised from their own educational process. Students reported that they were unable to gain the same depth of understanding in five subjects as they had had by concentrating on two subjects. They also reported difficulty in budgeting their time ("It's so difficult dealing with five subjects. Last year, I could really devote time to my two major subjects, but now I (often) spend too much time on one subject ... I use so much time on one that I end up neglecting the others.").

Many students complained that, relative to the previous two years, there was now no time or opportunity to get help in the Traditional classes. They were sharply critical of the structure of math classes, in which they said there was no opportunity to ask questions. The students were particularly sensitive to issues of class size, again especially in mathematics classes ("There are 30 kids in my Algebra (II) class, and you just can't get the help you need."). Many students viewed the teacher as unable to respond to the questions of individual students. They said that there was very little one-on-one help or any discussions in their classes this year, experiences that they viewed as a routine part of learning in the Renaissance format. Interestingly,

The Copernican Plan Evaluated

two students reported that the return to the Traditional program made it easier to "blend in with the class," and "easier to go through the day without being called on or challenged." These students talked about feeling powerless to make any changes in their current situation. They framed their discussion of school as "having to cope" with the process, and seemed to have little enthusiasm for coming to school. Without exception, students reported that their grades had declined with their return to the Traditional format. "I am doing worse, I don't understand things as well. Last year, I felt like I understood things for the test, this year I don't know what is really going on." All students said that they did not find the academic content to be more difficult, but rather that the format and techniques of the Traditional format made the material much more difficult to handle. All reported that tests and grading requirements were comparable relative to their Renaissance experience. They believed that their higher Renaissance grades were a function of greater understanding, not lower standards.

Fall, 1991: Videotaped Assessments of Higher Order Thinking Skills:

An investigation of differences between Renaissance students and Traditional students was made in the fall of 1991, with a focus on the possibility of differences in domain understanding, group collaboration, and dispositions of thinking (for more details, see Appendix G). This assessment occurred some five months after the Renaissance program had ended. Thirty-three students were videotaped as they worked in small groups on collaborative thought-provoking tasks. Half of these groups were assigned a science task, and half a history task. Half of the students were from Renpro and half from Tradpro.

Each science and history group was given a problem, and all students were asked to think about the problem for a few minutes, then share his or her ideas with the others. After these initial presentations, the students were asked to work together toward a final understanding of the problem, which they presented to the researchers.

Videotapes of each group were evaluated blind in terms of individual students' domain understanding, group collaboration, and thinking dispositions. Results of analyses indicated that, for the science groups, the quality of students' application of concepts of density in their thinking and evidence of their use of scientific inquiry varied according to whether they had been in Renpro or Tradpro: the former Renpro students exhibited significantly higher thinking and collaborative skills overall than did the Tradpro students. Similarly, for the history groups, former Renpro students exhibited significantly higher levels of sophistication in interpretations of historical facts and greater depth of historical understanding.

EPILOGUE

The Evaluation Team

It is not easy for us to close down this evaluation, knowing first that our time in Topsfield is coming to an end, but more importantly recognizing that an enormously significant effort to enlarge educational possibilities for students and teachers was terminated, even though the results were positive. The decision to end the Renaissance Program seemed to have been based more on financial and political considerations rather than educational ones. This evaluation supported a continuation of the program.

It is difficult to change schools even in the best of times. Instructional practices and schedules are the result of many deliberations over long periods of time. Any changes, structural or educational, are viewed with skepticism, and should be. But we know that schools can change, although the process is complicated.

As the program began, there was a major concern that students in the Renaissance program would not learn as much as students in the Traditional program. There was also a concern that the Renpro schedule would put students' learning at risk, for they might not retain as much: Renpro students had significantly fewer hours of class (100 vs. 139 hours in the first year; 118 vs. 139 hours in the second year, and 118 vs. 162 hours for science with the traditional laboratory period). While there were differences in scores between students in the two programs, these differences essentially balanced out. The results were comparable, even though there were significant differences in "time on task." In addition, Renpro students had more opportunities for academic enrichment (more courses, seminars, independent studies and FLEP programs) than did the Tradpro, and actually completed 13% more course credits than did Tradpro students. The Gap Tests, administered to determine levels of retention of course material over time, also showed that the Renaissance and the Traditional program students had comparable levels of retention. The Renaissance program met its academic objectives.

Because achievement scores were of particular interest, we focused much attention on these outcomes. Renaissance teachers felt that they were unable to take full advantage of the pedagogical changes they made in their instruction due to the constraints imposed by the achievement tests, which they knew were to be used to evaluate both programs. Possibly, more could have been learned about the benefits of the Renaissance program had such constraints not been present, and if achievement comparisons had not been so central to the evaluation.

A number of important differences were established through the surveys, interviews, and classroom observations: Renaissance students were better known by their teachers, were responded to with more care, did more writing, pursued issues in greater depth, enjoyed their classes more, felt more challenged, and gained deeper understandings. Oral exams assessing students' capacities for thinking through problems and working cooperatively showed that former Renaissance students performed significantly better than Traditional students on these dimensions. The students in the Renaissance program were enthusiastic about their experiences. Such responses should count.

We learned that students can move from classes of 46 minutes to those of 118 minutes and back again. They are more flexible when it comes to length of class than is normally assumed, although Renaissance students preferred the longer class periods. Concentration on only two classes in much longer periods, aided by reduced class size, markedly improves the interpersonal relationships that develop between teacher and student, and between student and student. Being able to focus on fewer topics brings more serious attention to these topics, and this appears to be highly beneficial to learning. Students who show little motivation toward things academic are more motivated in these classes. Providing students with constant opportunities for discussion of issues gives them ownership in the learning process they seldom acquire through lectures.

Another important factor emerged in the evaluation: Renaissance teachers were excited about their teaching. They felt rejuvenated and believed they were reaching students more productively than ever. We still recall — and will likely never forget — the reports of Renaissance teachers at the end of the first year during a meeting of the Masconomet Evaluation Committee. Veteran teachers spoke about their teaching with such energy that a retired teacher in the audience said "I am so enthusiastic about what I am hearing, I am sorry I am retired and not in the classroom." He went on to note, "I didn't feel that good about teaching at any point in my entire career." Such teacher responses should also count.

We learned that teachers of any level of seniority who get involved in developing a new program can become re-dedicated to teaching and give more time and energy to their students than previously. Simple changes in the length of class periods and in class size can in themselves invite teachers to re-think their pedagogical styles.

Are there subjects which are best taught in an intensive style and others which should be taught over longer periods? The statistical analyses of the achievement scores gives little conclusive evidence, and more research is needed. It may be that some subjects are better suited to the intensive mode, and that others fit the shorter class but continuous instructional pattern better. Possibly because the samples were small, simply analyzing the subjects by disciplinary structure did not shed light on this question.

The Renaissance Program was not perfect. Teachers were not particularly successful with seminars, they were just learning how to make cooperative learning groups more uniformly constructive, and there were some problems accommodating studies in foreign languages and the arts.

The demarkation between the two programs was too sharp. Students were too isolated in their respective academic studies. It has been recognized that, for students, school is a social as well as an academic experience. Unfortunately, the two programs were set up in opposition. This may not have been the intent, but students and their parents felt it and so did teachers. The evaluation process may have accentuated the competitiveness.

As one recounts positive outcomes of this exploration, one must remember that we should also learn from the mistakes that were made. The divisiveness between participants in both programs, including parents, school board members, even students, was most unfortunate. Some of the meetings between the two groups and some of the literature generated by the conflict seemed inappropriate. People have a right to support vigorously a position they believe in, but such support should be expressed in an educational manner. We hope that Masconomet will continue to carry an experimental banner in the future and that the "loyal opposition" will be watching every step.

Clearly American education, even at its best, is far from good enough. We must all strive to make it better, not with slogans or cliches, but by helping our children to learn better and more deeply. At the national level there is a large debate going on about the need to alter our approaches to teaching and learning and curricula. The Masconomet experiment will be one of the models to be considered, for it has contributed to the national discourse on school reform.

These results represent a small sample and only two years' experience, and thus cannot be viewed as conclusive. However, it is clear that the assumption that the traditional daily and yearly schedules are the more effective has been seriously challenged. Responsibility for justification now falls on those who favor the Traditional schedule. Implementing a Copernican style schedule can be accomplished with the expectation of favorable pedagogical outcomes.

The evaluation team wants to thank you for inviting us to join you in this venture. We have been most graciously received by students and their parents, by both Renpro and Tradpro teachers, by the administration, and by the evaluation committee. Some of us have long had a fondness for the North Shore which this venture has rekindled. Those new to the area joined us enthusiastically in this exciting experience. What could be better than to be engaged in trying to improve the quality of education with such good people.

Thank you.
The Evaluation Team[3]

Table 1
Midterm Examination Scores (1989–90)

Subject	Renaissance Program	Traditional Program	Significance
English-M	28.6 57	31.8 44	Significant (T)
English-E	43.2 57	39.7 44	Significant (R)
English-T	72.0 57	71.6 44	—
Algebra	49.5 44	46.1 32	Tendency (R)
Algebra 1A	55.7 16	55.9 12	—
Geometry	31.9 19	33.7 12	—
Social Studies	123.8 64	119.1 50	—
Science	90.8 36	92.0 52	Tendency (T)
Science Honors	43.3 14	49.0 16	Significant (T)
Spanish Intro	129.4 8	105.4 13	Significant (R)
Spanish & Honors	159.8 25	151.3 21	Significant (R)
German & Honors	73.9 11	78.1 14	—
French & Honors	141.6 25	139.2 13	—

Note: Statistical significance is not determined only by differences in group mean scores. The number of students enrolled in a class and the distribution of scores are important factors.

Table 1   135

Table 2
Final Examination Scores (1989–90)

Subject	Renaissance Program	Traditional Program	Significance
English-M	28.8 55	26.3 42	Significant (R)
English-E	45.3 55	45.5 42	—
English-T	74.1 55	71.8 42	—
Algebra	38.3 45	43.4 30	Significant (T)
Algebra 1A	26.6 16	25.9 10	—
Geometry	53.7 18	58.4 12	Tendency (T)
Social Studies	121.6 61	118.9 49	—
Science	112.3 66	115.7 52	—
Science Honors	53.3 14	43.4 17	Significant (R)
Spanish Intro	136.0 8	120.7 10	Tendency (R)
Spanish & Honors	139.0 25	134.0 20	—
German & Honors	58.9 12	74.0 14	—
French & Honors	87.2 25	93.0 13	—

Note: Statistical significance is not determined only by differences in group mean scores. The number of students enrolled in a class and the distribution of scores are important factors.

Table 3
Differences from Final Exams to Gap Tests (means adjusted for reading)

ENGLISH				
Program	**Final**	**Gap 1** (Sep)	**Gap 2** (Dec)	**Gap 3** (Mar)
Renaissance 1 N (months)	24.8 19	−4.9 19 (9)	−3.7 8 (12)	−1.7*d 8 (15)
Renaissance 2 N (months)	28.2 15	−5.7 14 (6)	−5.5 8 (9)	−9.2* 5 (12)
Renaissance 3 N (months)	25.4 20	−4.9 18 (3)	−4.0 8 (6)	−3.1 7 (9)
Traditional N (months)	26.2 43	−3.2 36 (3)	−4.1 19 (6)	−5.7 13 (9)

Note: All mean differences are significantly different from zero unless marked with a single asterisk. Those entries identified with a 'd' indicate a statistically significant difference between the Renaissance program and the Traditional program score changes.

Table 4
Differences from Final Exams to Gap Tests (means adjusted for reading)

ALGEBRA 1A				
Program	**Final**	**Gap 1** (Sep)	**Gap 2** (Dec)	**Gap 3** (Mar)
Renaissance 1 N (months)	27.2 15	−9.7 12 (9)	−10.0* 2 (12)	−10.2 6 (15)
Traditional N (months)	27.1 14	−3.4* 10 (3)	−10.0 4 (6)	4.1* 4 (9)

Note: All mean differences are significantly different from zero unless marked with a single asterisk. Those entries identified with a 'd' indicate a statistically significant difference between the Renaissance program and the Traditional program score changes.

Table 4 137

Table 5
Differences from Final Exams to Gap Tests (means adjusted for reading)

ALGEBRA 1				
Program	**Final**	**Gap 1** (Sep)	**Gap 2** (Dec)	**Gap 3** (Mar)
Renaissance 1 N (months)	41.7 11	−21.9d 10 (9)	−22.7 5 (12)	−24.1 5 (15)
Renaissance 2 N (months)	38.4 24	−15.1 21 (6)	−18.3 11 (9)	−14.4 10 (12)
Renaissance 3 N (months)	33.6d 10	−12.5 9 (3)	−16.7 5 (6)	−6.8*d 3 (9)
Traditional N (months)	43.4 29	−16.3 25 (3)	−19.8 13 (6)	−18.4 11 (9)

Note: All mean differences are significantly different from zero unless marked with a single asterisk. Those entries identified with a 'd' indicate a statistically significant difference between the Renaissance program and the Traditional program score changes.

Table 6
Differences from Final Exams to Gap Tests (means adjusted for reading)

GEOMETRY				
Program	**Final**	**Gap 1** (Sep)	**Gap 2** (Dec)	**Gap 3** (Mar)
Renaissance 3 N (months)	53.6 18	−9.7 18 (3)	−11.0d 9 (6)	−9.3 6 (9)
Traditional N (months)	58.6 12	−4.2 10 (3)	−3.7* 5 (6)	−14.0 4 (9)

Note: All mean differences are significantly different from zero unless marked with a single asterisk. Those entries identified with a 'd' indicate a statistically significant difference between the Renaissance program and the Traditional program score changes.

The Copernican Plan Evaluated

Table 7
Differences from Final Exams to Gap Tests (means adjusted for reading)

PHYSICAL SCIENCES			
Program	Final	Gap 2 (Dec)	Gap 3 (Mar)
Renaissance 1 N (months)	118.2 11	−34.5d 11 (9)	−34.9 10 (15)
Renaissance 2 N (months)	94.8d 5	−5.9* 5 (6)	−20.9* 3 (12)
Renaissance 3 N (months)	109.8 15	−25.7 15 (3)	−26.1 14 (9)
Traditional N (months)	114.4 23	−19.9 23 (3)	−26.6 19 (9)

Note: All mean differences are significantly different from zero unless marked with a single asterisk. Those entries identified with a 'd' indicate a statistically significant difference between the Renaissance program and the Traditional program score changes.

Table 8
Differences from Final Exams to Gap Tests (means adjusted for reading)

SOCIAL STUDIES			
Program	Final	Gap 1 (Sep)	Gap 2 (Dec)
Renaissance 1 N (months)	116.0 19	−36.4d 19 (9)	−38.2 11 (12)
Renaissance 2 N (months)	119.3 14	−31.4d 12 (6)	−36.6 5 (9)
Renaissance 3 N (months)	117.5 19	−24.6 17 (3)	−37.5 8 (6)
Traditional N (months)	118.9 49	−21.0 43 (3)	−35.3 16 (6)

Note: All mean differences are significantly different from zero unless marked with a single asterisk. Those entries identified with a 'd' indicate a statistically significant difference between the Renaissance program and the Traditional program score changes.

Table 8

Table 9
Midterm Exam Scores (1990–91)

NINTH GRADE				
Subject	**Ren 1**	**Ren 2**	**Ren 3**	**Trad**
English N	61.5 30			63.2 41
Algebra 1 N		50.0d 15		42.4 30
Algebra 1A N			53.6 12	56.6 8
Western Civ N	110.9 8		125.8 23	115.8 40
Physical Science N		71.2 12	82.2 18	74.5 37

Note: Those entries identified with a 'd' indicate a statistically significant difference between the Renaissance program and the Traditional program score changes.

Table 10
Midterm Exam Scores (1990–91)

NINTH GRADE				
Subject	**Ren 1**	**Ren 2**	**Ren 3**	**Trad**
English N	61.5d 30			56.3 100
Algebra 1 N		50.0d 15		35.0 60
Algebra 1A N			39.0 12	36.0 23
Western Civ N	110.9 8		109.8 21	115.1 87
Physical Science N		71.2d 12	106.1 17	102.1 77

Note: Those entries identified with a 'd' indicate a statistically significant difference between the Renaissance program and the Traditional program score changes.

Table 11
Midterm Exam Scores (1990–91) (means adjusted for reading)

TENTH GRADE				
Subject	**Ren 1**	**Ren 2**	**Ren 3**	**Trad**
English 10 N	59.8d 5	58.2d 5	49.5d 11	66.3 18
English 10H N		63.4 11	64.3 12	66.0 13
Algebra 1B N		46.0 11		44.0 6
Geometry N	46.3 15			46.8 10
History N	83.5 15	93.8 5		87.9 18
History H N	107.7 3	119.1 13	80.4 8	121.5 8
Biology N	113.4 17	135.0 8	123.7 7	126.0 15
Chemistry H N	49.5 15			50.0 8

Note: Those entries identified with a 'd' indicate a statistically significant difference between the Renaissance program and the Traditional program score changes.

Table 11   141

Table 12

Midterm Exam Scores (1990–91) (means adjusted for reading)

TENTH GRADE				
Subject	Ren 1	Ren 2	Ren 3	Trad
English 10 N	59.8 9	56.8 4	54.5d 12	64.6 80
English 10H N		67.3d 11	68.9d 13	76.5 28
Algebra 1B N		25.2 10		25.8 19
Geometry N	44.2 16		45.1 8	46.1 37
Trig N	24.5 8			25.8 19
History N	83.5d 15	93.8d 5	129.0 8	120.2 60
History H N	107.7 3	120.2 12		125.1 23
Biology N	113.4 17	135.0d 8	114.0 7	113.6 63
Chemistry H N	50.1 14			54.7 19

Note: Those entries identified with a 'd' indicate a statistically significant difference between the Renaissance program and the Traditional program score changes.

Appendix A

****

* Please write your name (last name, first name) and ID number in the space provided.

* If you are in the TRADITIONAL program, please fill in the "0" in column A.

* If you are in the RENAISSANCE program, please fill in the "0" in column B.

* Your answers will be known only to the Evaluation Team. Neither your parents nor your teachers will see your answers to this questionnaire.

* After you have completed the questionnaire, please feel free to use the space provided in the "Write-In Areas" to write any other feelings and comments you may have. Thank you.

****

* FOR THE QUESTIONS BELOW, PLEASE FILL IN THE APPROPRIATE CIRCLE ON THE DATA FORM. THANK YOU.

1. I feel that I can talk to my teacher(s) about any questions I may have about my schoolwork.
   A. Almost Always   B. Frequently   C. Some of the time   D. Rarely   E. Never

2. I feel that I can talk to my teacher(s) about things not related to schoolwork.
   A. Almost Always   B. Frequently   C. Some of the time   D. Rarely   E. Never

3. I feel my teachers individualize the classes to meet my specific academic needs.
   A. Almost Always   B. Frequently   C. Some of the time   D. Rarely   E. Never

4. I feel my teachers care about me.
   A. Strongly   B. Agree   C. Neither Agree   D. Disagree   E. Strongly
   Agree   nor Disagree   Disagree

5. I feel my teachers know me personally.
   A. Strongly   B. Agree   C. Neither Agree   D. Disagree   E. Strongly
   Agree   nor Disagree   Disagree

6. I get together with my classmates outside of school.
   A. Almost Always   B. Frequently   C. Some of the time   D. Rarely   E. Never

7. I get together with my classmates to work on projects for school.
   A. Almost Always   B. Frequently   C. Some of the time   D. Rarely   E. Never

8. I worry about my test scores/grades.
   A. Strongly   B. Agree   C. Neither Agree   D. Disagree   E. Strongly
   Agree   nor Disagree   Disagree

9. The amount of time I spend on my homework after school every day is...
   A. 0-30 minutes   B. 30 min.-1 hour   C. 1-2 hrs.   D. 2-3 hrs.   E.3hrs.or more

10. The amount of time I spend every day studying something which was not specifically assigned as homework is...
    A. 0-30 minutes   B. 30 min.-1 hour   C. 1-2 hrs.   D. 2-3 hrs.   E.3hrs.or more

11. I enjoy doing my homework.
    A. Almost Always   B. Frequently   C. Some of the time   D. Rarely   E. Never

12. I feel that I receive a consistent amount of homework every day. (As opposed to having none on one day, but a considerable amount the next day, etc.)
    A. Strongly   B. Agree   C. Neither Agree   D. Disagree   E. Strongly
    Agree   nor Disagree   Disagree

13. I feel responsible for my schoolwork.
    A. Strongly   B. Agree   C. Neither Agree   D. Disagree   E. Strongly
    Agree   nor Disagree   Disagree

14. I feel comfortable voicing my views, concerns or questions in class.
    A. Almost Always   B. Frequently   C. Some of the time   D. Rarely   E. Never

15. I feel comfortable in leading a discussion in class.
    A. Strongly   B. Agree   C. Neither Agree   D. Disagree   E. Strongly
       Agree   nor Disagree   Disagree

16. I discuss topics covered in class, outside of class, with my friends.
    A. Almost Always   B. Frequently   C. Some of the time   D. Rarely   E. Never

17. I discuss topics covered in class with family members.
    A. Almost Always   B. Frequently   C. Some of the time   D. Rarely   E. Never

18. My classes utilize materials taken from sources other than the textbook. (Worksheets, Videos, Films,
    Newspapers, etc.)
    A. Almost Always   B. Frequently   C. Some of the time   D. Rarely   E. Never

19. I feel challenged by my schoolwork.
    A. Almost Always   B. Frequently   C. Some of the time   D. Rarely   E. Never

20. Overall, I enjoy my school experience every day.
    A. Strongly   B. Agree   C. Neither Agree   D. Disagree   E. Strongly
       Agree   nor Disagree   Disagree

21. In general, I enjoy my teacher's lessons for class every day.
    A. Strongly   B. Agree   C. Neither Agree   D. Disagree   E. Strongly
       Agree   nor Disagree   Disagree

22. In my classes, I work in small groups.
    A. Almost Always   B. Frequently   C. Some of the time   D. Rarely   E. Never

23. In my classes, students give presentations.
    A. Almost Always   B. Frequently   C. Some of the time   D. Rarely   E. Never

24. We have class discussions.
    A. Almost Always   B. Frequently   C. Some of the time   D. Rarely   E. Never

25. My teachers lecture.
    A. Almost Always   B. Frequently   C. Some of the time   D. Rarely   E. Never

26. My teachers assign independent projects.
    A. Almost Always   B. Frequently   C. Some of the time   D. Rarely   E. Never

27. My teachers give us time to do homework in class.
    A. Almost Always   B. Frequently   C. Some of the time   D. Rarely   E. Never

28. Generally, I am satisfied with the amount of material that is covered in class every day.
    A. Strongly   B. Agree   C. Neither Agree   D. Disagree   E. Strongly
       Agree   nor Disagree   Disagree

29. Overall, I understand the material being taught in class.
    A. Strongly   B. Agree   C. Neither Agree   D. Disagree   E. Strongly
       Agree   nor Disagree   Disagree

30. Overall, I think the subjects covered in class are interesting.
    A. Strongly   B. Agree   C. Neither Agree   D. Disagree   E. Strongly
       Agree   nor Disagree   Disagree

31. In general, I feel that what I am learning in school is, or will someday be, useful.
    A. Strongly   B. Agree   C. Neither Agree   D. Disagree   E. Strongly
       Agree   nor Disagree   Disagree

32. I am satisfied with the amount of time I am able to spend with my friends in the other program.
    A. Strongly   B. Agree   C. Neither Agree   D. Disagree   E. Strongly
       Agree   nor Disagree   Disagree

33. The way it is set up, students in the Renaissance program get to know the students better than the students in the Traditional program.
    A. Strongly   B. Agree   C. Neither Agree   D. Disagree   E. Strongly
       Agree   nor Disagree   Disagree

34. In general, I am cautioned by my teacher(s), concerning behavior in class. (Talking, Being tardy, Eating, Cheating, Etc.)
    A. Almost Always   B. Frequently   C. Some of the time   D. Rarely E. Never

35. Scheduling has been a problem for me this year.
    A. Strongly   B. Agree   C. Neither Agree   D. Disagree   E. Strongly
       Agree   nor Disagree   Disagree

36. Do you have a job?
    A. Yes   B. No

37. If you have a job, how many hours a week do you work? (If you do not have a job, please leave this question blank).
    A. 0-5 hours   B. 5-10 hours   C. 10-15 hours   D. 15-20 hours   E. over 20 hours

38. How many hours a week do you spend on extracurricular activities? (If you are not involved in any extracurricular activities, please leave this question blank).
    A. 0-3 hours   B. 3-6 hours   C. 6-9 hours   D. 9-12 hours   E. over 12 hours

39. I participated in the decision to be in the program I am in.
    A. Strongly   B. Agree   C. Neither Agree   D. Disagree   E. Strongly
       Agree   nor Disagree   Disagree

40. If I had a choice as to which program to be in next year, I would choose...
    A. THE RENAISSANCE PROGRAM   B. THE TRADTIONAL PROGRAM

****

IF YOU ARE IN THE TRADITIONAL PROGRAM, PLEASE RESPOND TO THE SECTION BELOW. IF YOU ARE IN THE RENAISSANCE PROGRAM, PLEASE SKIP THIS SECTION AND LEAVE IT BLANK. THANK YOU.

****

41. I am satisfied with the Traditional program.
    A. Strongly   B. Agree   C. Neither Agree   D. Disagree   E. Strongly
       Agree   nor Disagree   Disagree

42. I am satisfied with the 50 minute class period.
    A. Strongly   B. Agree   C. Neither Agree   D. Disagree   E. Strongly
       Agree   nor Disagree   Disagree

43. In my opinion, the 50 minute classes seem to be a little too short at times.
    A. Strongly   B. Agree   C. Neither Agree   D. Disagree   E. Strongly
       Agree   nor Disagree   Disagree

****

IF YOU ARE IN THE RENAISSANCE PROGRAM, PLEASE RESPOND TO THE SECTION BELOW. IF YOU ARE IN THE TRADITIONAL PROGRAM, PLEASE SKIP THIS SECTION AND LEAVE IT BLANK. THANK YOU.

****

44. I am satisfied with the Renaissance program.
    A. Strongly   B. Agree   C. Neither Agree   D. Disagree   E. Strongly
       Agree   nor Disagree   Disagree

45. I am satisfied with the 100 minute class period.
    A. Strongly   B. Agree   C. Neither Agree   D. Disagree   E. Strongly
       Agree   nor Disagree   Disagree

Appendix A   145

46. In my opinion, the 100 minute classes seem to be just like two class periods put together.
   A. Strongly   B. Agree   C. Neither Agree   D. Disagree   E. Strongly
      Agree   nor Disagree   Disagree

* IF YOU HAVE NOT EXPERIENCED ANY OF THESE PROGRAMS YET, PLEASE LEAVE YOUR RESPONSES TO THE QUESTIONS BLANK.
  THANK YOU.

47. I enjoy my Seminar period.
   A. Strongly   B. Agree   C. Neither Agree   D. Disagree   E. Strongly
      Agree   nor Disagree   Disagree

48. I enjoy my FLEP period.
   A. Strongly   B. Agree   C. Neither Agree   D. Disagree   E. Strongly
      Agree   nor Disagree   Disagree

49. I enjoy my Independent Study period.
   A. Strongly   B. Agree   C. Neither Agree   D. Disagree   E. Strongly
      Agree   nor Disagree   Disagree

50. I am satisfied with my learning experience(s) in the Seminar program.
   A. Strongly   B. Agree   C. Neither Agree   D. Disagree   E. Strongly
      Agree   nor Disagree   Disagree

51. I am satisfied with my learning experience(s) in the FLEP program.
   A. Strongly   B. Agree   C. Neither Agree   D. Disagree   E. Strongly
      Agree   nor Disagree   Disagree

52. I am satisfied with my learning experience(s) in the Independent Study program.
   A. Strongly   B. Agree   C. Neither Agree   D. Disagree   E. Strongly
      Agree   nor Disagree   Disagree

53. I am satisfied with how FLEX time is being used.
   A. Strongly   B. Agree   C. Neither Agree   D. Disagree   E. Strongly
      Agree   nor Disagree   Disagree

54. I feel I have received valuable help during FLEX time.
   A. Strongly   B. Agree   C. Neither Agree   D. Disagree   E. Strongly
      Agree   nor Disagree   Disagree

55. I believe there has been a change in the teaching and learning processes in my classes.
   A. Strongly   B. Agree   C. Neither Agree   D. Disagree   E. Strongly
      Agree   nor Disagree   Disagree

56. I feel there has been a change in the responsiblity I feel for my own schoolwork and learning.
   A. Strongly   B. Agree   C. Neither Agree   D. Disagree   E. Strongly
      Agree   nor Disagree   Disagree

* After you have completed the questionnaire, please feel free to use the space provided in the "Write-In Areas"
  to write any other feelings and comments you may have. Thank you.

Appendix B

****

Response set: A = Almost every day
               B = About once a week
               C = About once a month
               D = A few times a year
               E = Never

****

1. My parents or guardian helped me with math homework.

2. My parents or guardian helped me with other homework.

3. My parents made me practice math over and over until I knew it.

4. My parents taught me to do extra problems not yet taught.

5. My parents say, "If you don't do well in school, you won't get into a good college."

6. My parents got a baby-sitter to look after me at home.

7. My parents say, "If you want to make a good living, get high marks in math and science."

8. My parents wouldn't let me do what I wanted until homework was finished.

9. My parents said they wanted to buy me things that would help with school, like workbooks, maps, calculators.

10. When I brought home good marks they said, "Good, but do better."

11. My parents said I could do better in school if I worked harder.

12. My parents made me feel ashamed if I did badly in school.

13. My parents used to tell about other students who are very good in school.

14. I could get out of doing some chore if I had homework to do.

15. My parents used to tell me when I could watch TV.

16. My parents used to tell me when I could go to friends' houses.

****

Response set: Y = Yes
               N = No

****

17. My parents gave me an allowance to spend the way I want.

18. My parents would always be angry if I had a fight with kids instead of ignoring them.

19. If they weren't sure my parents would ask if I had done my homework.

20. My parents would decide what I was allowed to do after school.

21. My mother thought that helping me with schoolwork was as important as her job or anything else she did.

22. My parents sacrificed for their kids' education all the time.

23. My parents sent me to summer school to learn extra stuff.

24. My parents rewarded me whenever I brought home good grades.

25. In high school, my parents give me an allowance to spend the way I want.

26. In high school, my parents ask whether I had done my homework.

27. In high school, my parents decide what I am allowed to do after school.

28. In high school, my parents sent me to summer school to learn extra stuff.

29. In high school, my parents reward me whenever I get good grades.

30. In high school, my parents let me hold a part-time job.

****

Response set: When you do well in math, it could be due to several reasons. Read each reason below, and rank order the four reasons. Put a "1" next to the most important reason, a "2" next to the second most important reason, a "3" next to the third most important reason, and a "4" next to the least important reason.

****

31. Effort, or how hard I try.

32. Natural ability, or how smart I am.

33. How easy the course work is.

34. How lucky I am.

****

Response set: When you do poorly in math, it could be due to several reasons. Read each reason below, and rank order the four reasons. Put a "1" next to the most important reason, a "2" next to the second most important reason, a "3" next to the third most important reason, and a "4" next to the least important reason.

****

35. Effort, or I didn't try hard enough.

36. Natural ability, or I'm not smart enough.

37. How difficult the course work is.

38. How unlucky I am.

****

Response set: A =   0% likely
                 B = 25% likely
                 C = 50% likely
                 D = 75% likely
                 E = 100% likely

****

39. How likely is it that someone could become smarter in the future?

40. How likely is it that someone could try harder in the future?

****

Response set: A = Very easy
                 B = Easy
                 C = Hard
                 D = Very hard

****

41. In your opinion, how easy or hard is mathematics?

****

Response set: A = Strongly Agree
                 B = Agree
                 C = Neutral
                 D = Disagree
                 E = Strongly Disagree

****

42. I enjoy mathematics.

43. I feel good when I solve a math problem on my own.

44. I would like to work at a job that lets me use mathematics.

45. I am good with numbers.

46. Most of mathematics has practical use.

47. Mathematics is useful in solving everyday problems.

48. Mathematics helps a person to think logically.

49. It's important to know mathematics in order to get a good job.

50. I really want to do well in mathematics.

51. I look forward to taking more mathematics.

Appendix C

****

* If you teach in the TRADITIONAL program, please fill in the "0" in column A.

* If you teach in the RENAISSANCE program, please fill in the "0" in column B.

* If you teach in BOTH programs, please fill in the "0" in column C, and answer the following questions in reference to your Renaissance classes.

* After you have completed the questionnaire, please feel free to use the space provided in the "Write-In Areas" to write any other feelings and comments you may have. Thank you.

****

* FOR THE QUESTIONS BELOW, PLEASE FILL IN THE APPROPRIATE CIRCLE ON THE DATA FORM. THANK YOU.

1. I am confident that my students will remember the most important elements of the material I am teaching.
   A. Strongly   B. Agree   C. Neither Agree   D. Disagree   E. Strongly
      Agree   nor Disagree   Disagree

2. I am confident that I will be able to cover the first half of the ninth grade syllabus by January.
   A. Strongly   B. Agree   C. Neither Agree   D. Disagree   E. Strongly
      Agree   nor Disagree   Disagree

3. I am satisfied that students are gaining a good understanding of the subject matter.
   A. Strongly   B. Agree   C. Neither Agree   D. Disagree   E. Strongly
      Agree   nor Disagree   Disagree

4. I am satisfied with the level of intellectual involvement of students in my class.
   A. Strongly   B. Agree   C. Neither Agree   D. Disagree   E. Strongly
      Agree   nor Disagree   Disagree

5. I am satisfied with the responsibility students take for their learning.
   A. Strongly   B. Agree   C. Neither Agree   D. Disagree   E. Strongly
      Agree   nor Disagree   Disagree

6. I am satisfied with the level of maturity of the ninth grade students.
   A. Strongly   B. Agree   C. Neither Agree   D. Disagree   E. Strongly
      Agree   nor Disagree   Disagree

7. I am satisfied that students are challenged to think independently.
   A. Strongly   B. Agree   C. Neither Agree   D. Disagree   E. Strongly
      Agree   nor Disagree   Disagree

8. I am satisfied by the level of interest shown by students in their education.
   A. Strongly   B. Agree   C. Neither Agree   D. Disagree   E. Strongly
      Agree   nor Disagree   Disagree

9. I am satisfied with the quality of my relationships with students.
   A. Strongly   B. Agree   C. Neither Agree   D. Disagree   E. Strongly
      Agree   nor Disagree   Disagree

10. I am able to assess my students' needs to my satisfaction.
    A. Strongly   B. Agree   C. Neither Agree   D. Disagree   E. Strongly
       Agree   nor Disagree   Disagree

11. I am confident I know the strengths and weaknesses of each of my students.
    A. Strongly   B. Agree   C. Neither Agree   D. Disagree   E. Strongly
       Agree   nor Disagree   Disagree

12. I am satisfied with the flexibility in the curriculum to adjust for individual student needs.
   A. Strongly   B. Agree   C. Neither Agree   D. Disagree   E. Strongly
      Agree   nor Disagree   Disagree

13. I am satisfied with the thoroughness with which students complete their homework.
   A. Strongly   B. Agree   C. Neither Agree   D. Disagree   E. Strongly
      Agree   nor Disagree   Disagree

14. Students initiate discussions.
   A. Almost Always   B. Frequently   C. Some of the time   D. Rarely   E. Never

15. How many hours a day, on average, do you expect your students to spend on homework?
   A. 0-30 minutes   B. 30 min.-1 hour   C. 1-2 hrs.   D. 2-3 hrs.   E. 3hrs.or more

16. How much of what is taught do you expect students to remember three years from now?
   A. 0-20%   B. 20%-40%   C. 40%-70%   D. 70%-85%   E. 85%-100%

17. How many times a week do you use group activities in your classes?
   A. 0-1   B. 2-3   C. 4-6   D. 7-9   E. 10 or more

18. I am satisfied with the amount of interaction I have with my colleagues.
   A. Strongly   B. Agree   C. Neither Agree   D. Disagree   E. Strongly
      Agree   nor Disagree   Disagree

19. I am satisfied with the amount of staff development available to me as a teacher.
   A. Strongly   B. Agree   C. Neither Agree   D. Disagree   E. Strongly
      Agree   nor Disagree   Disagree

20. I am satisfied with the quantity of interaction between administration and staff.
   A. Strongly   B. Agree   C. Neither Agree   D. Disagree   E. Strongly
      Agree   nor Disagree   Disagree

21. I am satisfied with the amount of input I have in school decisions.
   A. Strongly   B. Agree   C. Neither Agree   D. Disagree   E. Strongly
      Agree   nor Disagree   Disagree

22. I am satisfied with the level of support and encouragement I have received for my teaching program.
   A. Strongly   B. Agree   C. Neither Agree   D. Disagree   E. Strongly
      Agree   nor Disagree   Disagree

23. Overall, I am satisfied with the quality of my exeriences as an educator.
   A. Strongly   B. Agree   C. Neither Agree   D. Disagree   E. Strongly
      Agree   nor Disagree   Disagree

24. The subject matter I teach is respected.
   A. Strongly   B. Agree   C. Neither Agree   D. Disagree   E. Strongly
      Agree   nor Disagree   Disagree

25. I am satisfied with the amount of time provided for planning.
   A. Strongly   B. Agree   C. Neither Agree   D. Disagree   E. Strongly
      Agree   nor Disagree   Disagree

26. I am satisfied with the amount of time provided for meetings with colleagues.
   A. Strongly   B. Agree   C. Neither Agree   D. Disagree   E. Strongly
      Agree   nor Disagree   Disagree

27. I am satisfied with the level of parental involvement.
   A. Strongly   B. Agree   C. Neither Agree   D. Disagree   E. Strongly
      Agree   nor Disagree   Disagree

28. I am satisfied that students, generally, are learning as much as they should this academic year.
   A. Strongly   B. Agree   C. Neither Agree   D. Disagree   E. Strongly
      Agree   nor Disagree   Disagree

29. I am satisfied with the sizes of my classes.
   A. Strongly   B. Agree   C. Neither Agree   D. Disagree   E. Strongly
      Agree   nor Disagree   Disagree

30. I carry a fair workload.
    A. Strongly   B. Agree   C. Neither Agree   D. Disagree   E. Strongly
       Agree   nor Disagree   Disagree

31. How did you feel about the Renaissance Program six months ago?
    A. Very Positive   B. Positive   C. Neutral   D. Negative   E. Very Negative

32. How do you feel about the Renaissance Program now?
    A. Very Positive   B. Positive   C. Neutral   D. Negative   E. Very Negative

33. I am satisfied with the manner in which information about the Renaissance program was disseminated.
    A. Strongly   B. Agree   C. Neither Agree   D. Disagree   E. Strongly
       Agree   nor Disagree   Disagree

34. I am concerned that the Renaissance Program may eventually be a threat to my job.
    A. Strongly   B. Agree   C. Neither Agree   D. Disagree   E. Strongly
       Agree   nor Disagree   Disagree

****

IF YOU TEACH IN THE RENAISSANCE PROGRAM, PLEASE RESPOND TO THE SECTION BELOW. IF YOU TEACH IN THE TRADITIONAL PROGRAM, PLEASE SKIP THIS SECTION AND LEAVE IT BLANK. THANK YOU.

****

35. I am satisfied with the quality of the learning experience of seminars.
    A. Strongly   B. Agree   C. Neither Agree   D. Disagree   E. Strongly
       Agree   nor Disagree   Disagree

36. I am satisfied with the quality of the learning experience of Independent Study.
    A. Strongly   B. Agree   C. Neither Agree   D. Disagree   E. Strongly
       Agree   nor Disagree   Disagree

37. I am satisfied with the quality of the learning experience of FLEP.
    A. Strongly   B. Agree   C. Neither Agree   D. Disagree   E. Strongly
       Agree   nor Disagree   Disagree

38. I am satisfied with the use of FLEX time.
    A. Strongly   B. Agree   C. Neither Agree   D. Disagree   E. Strongly
       Agree   nor Disagree   Disagree

39. I feel there is a consistent set of criteria for the work I give to my honors students.
    A. Strongly   B. Agree   C. Neither Agree   D. Disagree   E. Strongly
       Agree   nor Disagree   Disagree

* PLEASE ANSWER THE FOLLOWING ONLY IF YOU TEACH HONORS STUDENTS.

40. I am satisfied with the quality of work my honors students complete.
    A. Strongly   B. Agree   C. Neither Agree   D. Disagree   E. Strongly
       Agree   nor Disagree   Disagree

41. I am skeptical about the honors work given by the other Renaissance program teachers.
    A. Strongly   B. Agree   C. Neither Agree   D. Disagree   E. Strongly
       Agree   nor Disagree   Disagree

* After you have completed the questionnaire, please feel free to use the space provided in the "Write-In Areas" to write any other feelings and comments you may have. Thank you.

Appendix D

****

* If your child is in the TRADITIONAL program, please fill in the "0" in column A.

* If your child is in the RENAISSANCE program, please fill in the "0" in column B.

* After you have completed the questionnaire, please feel free to use the space provided in the "Write-In Areas" to write any other feelings and comments you may have. Thank you.

****

* FOR THE QUESTIONS BELOW, PLEASE FILL IN THE APPROPRIATE CIRCLE ON THE DATA FORM. THANK YOU.

1. Person responding is...
   A. Mother   B. Father   C. Stepmother   D. Stepfather   E. Other
                                                                                (legal guardian)

2. Information about the Renaissance Program was communicated in a timely way last year.
   A. Strongly   B. Agree   C. Neither Agree   D. Disagree   E. Strongly
      Agree   nor Disagree   Disagree

3. Information disseminated last year about the logistics of the Renaissance Program was clear (i.e. How it would work).
   A. Strongly   B. Agree   C. Neither Agree   D. Disagree   E. Strongly
      Agree   nor Disagree   Disagree

4. Information about the implications of the Renaissance Program for my child's future education (i.e. college) was clear.
   A. Strongly   B. Agree   C. Neither Agree   D. Disagree   E. Strongly
      Agree   nor Disagree   Disagree

5. I am satisfied with the way the school is communicating to parents the progress of the Renaissance Program.
   A. Strongly   B. Agree   C. Neither Agree   D. Disagree   E. Strongly
      Agree   nor Disagree   Disagree

6. Knowing what I know now, I would still allow my child to make the same decisions about whether or not to enroll in the Renaissance Program this year.
   A. Strongly   B. Agree   C. Neither Agree   D. Disagree   E. Strongly
      Agree   nor Disagree   Disagree

7. I am satisfied with my child's school performance thus far this year.
   A. Strongly   B. Agree   C. Neither Agree   D. Disagree   E. Strongly
      Agree   nor Disagree   Disagree

8. I am satisfied with my child's attitudes toward his or her schoolwork this year.
   A. Strongly   B. Agree   C. Neither Agree   D. Disagree   E. Strongly
      Agree   nor Disagree   Disagree

* FOR QUESTIONS #8-#19, IF YOUR CHILD HAS NOT EXPERIENCED ANY OF THESE CLASSES YET, PLEASE LEAVE YOUR RESPONSES TO THE QUESTIONS BLANK. THANK YOU.

9. I am satisfied with the way in which math is being taught this year.
   A. Strongly   B. Agree   C. Neither Agree   D. Disagree   E. Strongly
      Agree   nor Disagree   Disagree

10. I am satisfied with the way English is being taught this year.
    A. Strongly   B. Agree   C. Neither Agree   D. Disagree   E. Strongly
       Agree   nor Disagree   Disagree

11. I am satisfied with the way Western Civilization is being taught this year.
    A. Strongly   B. Agree   C. Neither Agree   D. Disagree   E. Strongly
       Agree   nor Disagree   Disagree

12. I am satisfied with the way science is being taught this year.
    A. Strongly   B. Agree   C. Neither Agree   D. Disagree   E. Strongly
       Agree   nor Disagree   Disagree

13. I am satisfied with the way art is being taught this year.
    A. Strongly   B. Agree   C. Neither Agree   D. Disagree   E. Strongly
       Agree   nor Disagree   Disagree

14. I am satisfied with the way Computers is being taught this year.
    A. Strongly   B. Agree   C. Neither Agree   D. Disagree   E. Strongly
       Agree   nor Disagree   Disagree

15. My child is satisfied with his/her math teacher this year.
    A. Strongly   B. Agree   C. Neither Agree   D. Disagree   E. Strongly
       Agree   nor Disagree   Disagree

16. My child is happy with his/her English teacher this year.
    A. Strongly   B. Agree   C. Neither Agree   D. Disagree   E. Strongly
       Agree   nor Disagree   Disagree

17. My child is happy with his/her Western Civilization teacher this year.
    A. Strongly   B. Agree   C. Neither Agree   D. Disagree   E. Strongly
       Agree   nor Disagree   Disagree

18. My child is happy with his/her science teacher this year.
    A. Strongly   B. Agree   C. Neither Agree   D. Disagree   E. Strongly
       Agree   nor Disagree   Disagree

19. My child is happy with his/her art teacher this year.
    A. Strongly   B. Agree   C. Neither Agree   D. Disagree   E. Strongly
       Agree   nor Disagree   Disagree

20. My child is happy with his/her Computer teacher this year.
    A. Strongly   B. Agree   C. Neither Agree   D. Disagree   E. Strongly
       Agree   nor Disagree   Disagree

21. I would support my child's decision to enroll in the Renaissance Program next year.
    A. Yes   B. No

22. The decision about whether or not my child should enroll in the Renaissance Program was a source of tension
    in my family.
    A. Strongly   B. Agree   C. Neither Agree   D. Disagree   E. Strongly
       Agree   nor Disagree   Disagree

23. Compared to last year, I see improvements this year in my child's general attitude toward school.
    A. Strongly   B. Agree   C. Neither Agree   D. Disagree   E. Strongly
       Agree   nor Disagree   Disagree

24. I see improvements this year in my child's general satisfaction with school.
    A. Strongly   B. Agree   C. Neither Agree   D. Disagree   E. Strongly
       Agree   nor Disagree   Disagree

25. My perception is that the best ninth grade teachers are in the Renaissance Program.
    A. Strongly   B. Agree   C. Neither Agree   D. Disagree   E. Strongly
       Agree   nor Disagree   Disagree

26. I am satisfied that my child's individual needs are being met.
    A. Strongly   B. Agree   C. Neither Agree   D. Disagree   E. Strongly
       Agree   nor Disagree   Disagree

27. I feel the teachers know my child well.
    A. Strongly   B. Agree   C. Neither Agree   D. Disagree   E. Strongly
       Agree   nor Disagree   Disagree

28. I am satisfied with the depth of instruction.
    A. Strongly   B. Agree   C. Neither Agree   D. Disagree   E. Strongly
       Agree   nor Disagree   Disagree

29. My child takes reponsibility for his/her own learning.
   A. Strongly   B. Agree   C. Neither Agree   D. Disagree   E. Strongly
      Agree   nor Disagree   Disagree

30. I am satisfied with the amount of homework my child receives.
   A. Strongly   B. Agree   C. Neither Agree   D. Disagree   E. Strongly
      Agree   nor Disagree   Disagree

31. I am satisfied with my child's class sizes.
   A. Strongly   B. Agree   C. Neither Agree   D. Disagree   E. Strongly
      Agree   nor Disagree   Disagree

* After you have completed the questionnaire, please feel free to use the space provided in the "Write-In Areas" to write any other feelings and comments you may have. Thank you.

Appendix E

Good Evening. My name is _____. I am calling you on behalf of the Masconomet Evaluation Team. I hope you received our letter asking you for your participation in this telephone survey. (If no: I have a copy here, may I read it to you?) Is this a good time to talk? It will take about 10 minutes.

1. What do you see as the general highlights/strengths of the program in which your child participates? (i.e. class size, motivation, enthusiasm, improved grades, relationships with students and teachers…)

2. What are your major concerns about the program your child is in?

3. Do you feel that the program is meeting your child's needs in terms of your educational aspirations for him/her? In what ways does the program meet your hopes for your child's education and future?

4. Overall, how would you rate the child's experience of being enrolled in the Renaissance/Traditional program this year?

Appendix F

1.-2. In the appropriate space for questions 1 and 2, please indicate the subject you teach:
   1A. Mathematics   1B. English   1C. Social Studies   1D. Science   1E. Foreign Language
   2A. Special Education   2B. Art/Music   2C. Physical Education   2D. Other

3. Have you taught in the Renaissance program?
   A. No.   B. Yes, for the past two years.   C. Yes, this year only.   D. Yes, last year only.

4. Students currently in the Renaissance program should be allowed to complete high school in Renaissance.
   A. Strongly   B. Agree   C. Neither Agree   D. Disagree   E. Strongly
      Agree   nor Disagree   Disagree

5. The Traditional format of 45 minute classes over 180 days is conducive to quality education.
   A. Strongly   B. Agree   C. Neither Agree   D. Disagree   E. Strongly
      Agree   nor Disagree   Disagree

6. A class format of double period classes every other day is conducive to quality education.
   A. Strongly   B. Agree   C. Neither Agree   D. Disagree   E. Strongly
      Agree   nor Disagree   Disagree

7. A class format of double period classes every day for one semester is conducive to quality education.
   A. Strongly   B. Agree   C. Neither Agree   D. Disagree   E. Strongly
      Agree   nor Disagree   Disagree

8. The Renaissance format is conducive to quality education.
   A. Strongly   B. Agree   C. Neither Agree   D. Disagree   E. Strongly
      Agree   nor Disagree   Disagree

9. Renaissance presents no problems in my discipline, but I worry about its effects on instruction in other subjects.
   A. Strongly   B. Agree   C. Neither Agree   D. Disagree   E. Strongly
      Agree   nor Disagree   Disagree

10. Renaissance offers an advantage for foreign language instruction because it allows for instruction through immersion.
    A. Strongly   B. Agree   C. Neither Agree   D. Disagree   E. Strongly
       Agree   nor Disagree   Disagree

11. During the past two years, Traditional teachers were made to feel "less valued" at Masconomet High School.
    A. Strongly   B. Agree   C. Neither Agree   D. Disagree   E. Strongly
       Agree   nor Disagree   Disagree

12. "Getting to know our students better" should be a goal of the teaching staff.
    A. Strongly   B. Agree   C. Neither Agree   D. Disagree   E. Strongly
       Agree   nor Disagree   Disagree

13. Renaissance teachers have lower standards in their classes and their grades are inflated.
    A. Strongly   B. Agree   C. Neither Agree   D. Disagree   E. Strongly
       Agree   nor Disagree   Disagree

14. The worst feature of the Renaissance experiment was the division of the school.
    A. Strongly   B. Agree   C. Neither Agree   D. Disagree   E. Strongly
       Agree   nor Disagree   Disagree

15. The "team" concept, used in junior high, should be expanded to the high school whenever possible.
    A. Strongly   B. Agree   C. Neither Agree   D. Disagree   E. Strongly
       Agree   nor Disagree   Disagree

16. Masconomet is an excellent school; "if it ain't broke, don't fix it."
    A. Strongly   B. Agree   C. Neither Agree   D. Disagree   E. Strongly
       Agree   nor Disagree   Disagree

17. The Renaissance program is a threat to the honors program at Masconomet.
    A. Strongly   B. Agree   C. Neither Agree   D. Disagree   E. Strongly
       Agree   nor Disagree   Disagree

18. Using the same midterm and final examinations in Renaissance and Traditional classes resulted in less
    effective instruction.
    A. Strongly   B. Agree   C. Neither Agree   D. Disagree   E. Strongly
       Agree   nor Disagree   Disagree

19. I prefer to teach the same courses every year.
    A. Strongly   B. Agree   C. Neither Agree   D. Disagree   E. Strongly
       Agree   nor Disagree   Disagree

20. Because Renaissance schedules two blocks every trimester, the students are encouraged to take more major
    classes.
    A. Strongly   B. Agree   C. Neither Agree   D. Disagree   E. Strongly
       Agree   nor Disagree   Disagree

21. There is not enough time for teachers to talk to each other about professional concerns.
    A. Strongly   B. Agree   C. Neither Agree   D. Disagree   E. Strongly
       Agree   nor Disagree   Disagree

22. It will take a long time to heal the divisions caused by the Renaissance program.
    A. Strongly   B. Agree   C. Neither Agree   D. Disagree   E. Strongly
       Agree   nor Disagree   Disagree

23. 45 minute periods restrict my ability to do a good job.
    A. Strongly   B. Agree   C. Neither Agree   D. Disagree   E. Strongly
       Agree   nor Disagree   Disagree

24. Using lectures as a predominant teaching style is too prevalent at Masconomet High School.
    A. Strongly   B. Agree   C. Neither Agree   D. Disagree   E. Strongly
       Agree   nor Disagree   Disagree

25. Political considerations were responsible for the demise of the Renaissance program.
    A. Strongly   B. Agree   C. Neither Agree   D. Disagree   E. Strongly
       Agree   nor Disagree   Disagree

26. Masconomet should continue to offer both Renaissance and Traditional options for its students.
    A. Strongly   B. Agree   C. Neither Agree   D. Disagree   E. Strongly
       Agree   nor Disagree   Disagree

27. It would be better to have an all Renaissance school rather than return to an all Traditional format.
    A. Strongly   B. Agree   C. Neither Agree   D. Disagree   E. Strongly
       Agree   nor Disagree   Disagree

28. We should be moving to a middle ground between Renaissance and Traditional formats.
    A. Strongly   B. Agree   C. Neither Agree   D. Disagree   E. Strongly
       Agree   nor Disagree   Disagree

29. The Renaissance format is more conducive to student-teacher rapport.
    A. Strongly   B. Agree   C. Neither Agree   D. Disagree   E. Strongly
       Agree   nor Disagree   Disagree

30. Renaissance reduces retention problems.
    A. Strongly   B. Agree   C. Neither Agree   D. Disagree   E. Strongly
       Agree   nor Disagree   Disagree

31. The administration is generally supportive of the teaching staff.
    A. Strongly   B. Agree   C. Neither Agree   D. Disagree   E. Strongly
       Agree   nor Disagree   Disagree

32. Renaissance classes are less rigorous than Traditional classes.
    A. Strongly   B. Agree   C. Neither Agree   D. Disagree   E. Strongly
       Agree   nor Disagree   Disagree

33. If my child were a student at Masconomet, and both programs were scheduled to run for the next four years, I would:
   A. Insist that my child be placed in Renaissance.
   B. Encourage my child to choose Renaissance.
   C. Be neutral and allow my child to choose.
   D. Encourage my child to choose the Traditional program.
   E. Insist that my child be placed in the Traditional program.

34. Mathematics cannot be successfully taught in the Renaissance format.
   A. Strongly   B. Agree   C. Neither Agree   D. Disagree   E. Strongly
      Agree   nor Disagree   Disagree

35. There is a "Phase II Problem" at Masconomet that needs to be addressed.
   A. Strongly   B. Agree   C. Neither Agree   D. Disagree   E. Strongly
      Agree   nor Disagree   Disagree

36. My friendships and relationships among Masconomet teachers have been changed by the Renaissance program.
   A. Strongly   B. Agree   C. Neither Agree   D. Disagree   E. Strongly
      Agree   nor Disagree   Disagree

37. My teaching preference is:
   A. Grades 7-8   B. Grade 9   C. Grade 10   D. Grade 11-12   E. No preference

38. The administration often makes major decisions without consulting the teaching staff.
   A. Strongly   B. Agree   C. Neither Agree   D. Disagree   E. Strongly
      Agree   nor Disagree   Disagree

39. The Renaissance program improved the attitudes of the students in the program.
   A. Strongly   B. Agree   C. Neither Agree   D. Disagree   E. Strongly
      Agree   nor Disagree   Disagree

40. I would like to teach a new or different course next year.
   A. Strongly   B. Agree   C. Neither Agree   D. Disagree   E. Strongly
      Agree   nor Disagree   Disagree

41. The Renaissance program is responsible for an increase of discipline problems among its students.
   A. Strongly   B. Agree   C. Neither Agree   D. Disagree   E. Strongly
      Agree   nor Disagree   Disagree

42. Conducting two programs was too expensive, so it was budget considerations that forced the elimination of the Renaissance program.
   A. Strongly   B. Agree   C. Neither Agree   D. Disagree   E. Strongly
      Agree   nor Disagree   Disagree

43. The evaluation process has been helpful in understanding the strengths and weaknesses of the Renaissance program.
   A. Strongly   B. Agree   C. Neither Agree   D. Disagree   E. Strongly
      Agree   nor Disagree   Disagree

44. The evaluation process can improve Masconomet if the strengths of the Renaissance program are incorporated into the regular school program.
   A. Strongly   B. Agree   C. Neither Agree   D. Disagree   E. Strongly
      Agree   nor Disagree   Disagree

45. For Renaissance teachers only: If I had it to do over again, I would have taught in the Renaissance program.
   A. Strongly   B. Agree   C. Neither Agree   D. Disagree   E. Strongly
      Agree   nor Disagree   Disagree

46. For Traditional teachers only: I would have liked an opportunity to teach in the Renaissance program.
   A. Strongly   B. Agree   C. Neither Agree   D. Disagree   E. Strongly
      Agree   nor Disagree   Disagree

Thank you for your participation in this survey.
The Evaluation Team

Appendix F

Appendix G

Letter to the Masconomet School Committee

David Donavel, Renaissance Program Coordinator
and the Renaissance Program Teachers

DATE: September 28, 1990

TO: Masconomet School Committee

FROM: David Donavel, Renaissance Program Coordinator

RE: Renaissance Program, School Year 1991-92

As you consider the future of the Renaissance Program, I urge you to take into account the attached statement about teaching and learning in that new structure. We offer this as an honest, professional, and independent judgment about our experience over the past year and some weeks of teaching. Thanks for your time and thoughtfulness in making some difficult decisions.

Teaching in the Renaissance Structure

While it is still too early to come to solid conclusions about the effectiveness of teaching and learning in the Renaissance Program, we feel it necessary to state as clearly as we can now the ways in which we think the Renaissance structure is superior to the Traditional structure. Our urgency grows out of the fact that many powerful people in our community, both in and outside the school, have already reached opposite conclusions. Indeed, some of those people reached the conclusion that a Renaissance or Copernican structure is unworkable as early as 1983 and seem unmoved by the mounting evidence that they were wrong.

The advantages the Renaissance structure has over the traditional structure are:

1. Teachers are more able to individualize instruction so as to meet the learning needs of ALL students—not just those at the "top" or the "bottom." Because of that close monitoring of and adjustment for student progress or lack thereof, more able students get less bored; less able students get less discouraged.

2. Students can concentrate on their disciplines to a degree that's not possible when they have many subjects to which they must attend. Because of that sustained focus, students see more easily that monosyllabic answers to complex questions will not do. Because of the difference in pace in a Renaissance class, students are more patient with difficult problems than are their counterparts in the Traditional program. Consequently, they like learning better.

3. Students tend to feel they have a greater stake in their education. They do homework more willingly; they pay attention in class more willingly; they think more willingly; and they have less tolerance of busy work and poor teaching.

4. Students learn as much in a Renaissance structure as their counterparts do in less time. The Renaissance Program is more efficient. We know that from the testing we've done. Whether what they learn is enough or is what they should be learning or represents all they can learn are different and important questions. Right now, we know they can do what's been done in the Traditional program.

These are critically important superiorities. Moreover, we see no areas in which the Traditional structure can claim, at this point, to be superior. It is not as if we're "trading" gains in the areas mentioned here at the expense of some other equally important areas. So the gains we're making are not "expensive" in that sense. That too is critically important.

During the first year of the Renaissance Program there was a tendency on the part of the factions that developed in the community to identify teachers as either RenPro or TradPro teachers and to identify students in the same way. That was probably unavoidable. It was, however, inaccurate. With one exception, those of us in the Renaissance Program have been at Masconomet for many years. We are not inexperienced "hot shots" from some clever school of education coming out to show folks how it's done. We are TradPro teachers. We know the Traditional Program as well as anyone. We also do not see ourselves in competition with anyone—and especially not the "TradPro" teachers. We are trying out an idea and we can, at this early date, reach the conclusions cited above. Later on we'll have new conclusions and will have refined those. Right now, we are pretty certain that what we've said about the superiority of this program is accurate.

Furthermore, the Renaissance Program is not an implied criticism of any person or set of people. The program is a way for teachers to succeed at teaching—all teachers. Ironically, teachers critical of the program have said that if they had small classes they too could achieve improved results. No one doubts that. They could achieve improved results because they would enjoy improved contact with the students, and because they could individualize instruction. But merely reducing class size will not be enough, even it were affordable. Teachers need a dramatically reduced student load and both students and teachers need time to think, and teach, and learn and time to get to know one another. Unfortunately, no one wants to pay for traditionally structured classes no larger than 15. We do not have enough money for each kid to be known well by an adult in the school in a traditional structure. The Renaissance structure makes us able to afford it. We have no doubt that those teachers critical of the program could acheive fine results in it—they are good teachers.

We want to underscore, too the truth that this is not a program or structure for the academically disabled. There is no evidence that a Renaissance structure would not be as superior for honors students as it has been for our "Phase II" students. Indeed, Masconomet has a history of making special accommodations for our most able and largely that has meant instruction tailored to individual needs, sometimes in the shape of special tutorials and sometimes in the shape of smaller classes. It is ironic that much of the criticism of the program has come from the parents of honors students since the Renaissance Program would seem to provide the chance for those children to move ahead rapidly under the close supervision of a good teacher—precisely the chance that people are willing to pay for when they send their children to private schools.

Before we started in September of 1989 there were a good deal of dire predictions made about why the structure would never work. Here are some: Kids can't sit for 100 minutes. You can't cover the material in that amount of time. When kids are absent, they'll never catch up. When teachers are absent, the program will collapse. Kids won't do the homework necessary. The seminars will never work. Except for the last one, none of those proved accurate. That the seminars were not successful is due, we think, largely to poor planning and not to a fault in the concept. We hope for a chance to try again. People are still making predictions, but, necessarily fewer of them and, interestingly, the awful consequences of the program, according to the predictors, will only be seen later on. The new set: Kids will never remember what they're taught. Kids will be overwhelmed in college. There may be others. Our sense is that like the first batch, these too will not be borne out by experience. And yet, while the predictions fail to come true, the feelings about the program seem to run higher and higher. We wonder why. If there is something wrong with the teaching and learning within the program, no one has made it clear what that is. *And the merits of the program MUST be determined on the basis of teaching and learning. Nothing else matters.*

Is the Renaissance Program perfect? Is it the final answer to what ails the American high school? Is it the final answer to what ails Masconomet? NO. It's a structure that's superior to the one it's replacing. It's a structure that allows for better teaching and improved learning. There is much wrong with it. It may not be bold enough. We need to re-focus our curricula on higher-order skills and find ways to successfully demand students think harder and more clearly. We need to improve the seminars and independent study pieces. We need to clearly articulate the goals we have for our students—throughout the school. We need to find ways to get teachers less busy so they too can think and find ways to improve their own performance in class. There's much to be done.

The question, of course, for the School Committee is "Do we continue this program?" There are many reasons why dropping it would seem more comfortable. It's difficult to start new programs in a dismal economic climate. It's difficult to listen to angry constituents. It's easy to get complacent about how good Masconomet is already. And it's pleasant to imagine that if there were no Renaissance Program, we could pull together once more, share common goals, and maybe effectively address the economic crisis that continues to grow. But if we toss out the program, we haven't by doing so tossed out the problems that lead to it in the first place. Here's a helpful anecdote: On the summer reading reports we ask our students to complete during the first day or two of school, this fall one TradPro sophomore stated that he'd read a book called *Getting Straight A's*. He writes in his report: "I liked it because he explains some ways to become a better student and not become an outcast." To those who think we should abandon the Renaissance Program, we ask, what are you planning to do about that sad response? What are you planning to do about the fact that even Masco students are ashamed to use their brains? What are you planning to do?

That the Renaissance Program has gained enough attention nationally to be cited in the July 9, 1990 *U.S. News and World Report's* survey entitled "The Best of America" suggests that what we are doing is both important and needed. Last spring educators came from all over the country to talk with us. They left excited. When some of us visited schools in Washington and Florida and Wyoming to talk about the program, teachers and administrators were excited. We think the program is potentially powerful. Already it is an important national model for high school restructuring. Does Masconomet owe the country an experiment? We think it does. Former U.S. Secretary of Labor William Brock said a few years ago that this country had about ten years to get in shape educationally if it wanted to maintain its competitive place among industrialized nations. Other school reform efforts elsewhere seem not to have substantially improved student learning. The public is impatient. Business is impatient. A school structured for a world and economy that passed away twenty years ago will no longer do. The Renaissance Program seems to have tremendous potential to improve student outcomes, and in a very real sense, contribute to solving a national crisis. As such, it needs a trial. We're trying it here. We hope we can continue.

David Donavel	Lee Thomas	Jack Paarlberg
Dick Craig	Chuck Hodsdon	Don Doliber
Charlie McClory	Joe Czarnecki	Denise Eschenbach
Rob Manning	Vija Skudra	Andy Martinez

Appendix H

An Investigation of Students' Domain Understanding,
Group Collaboration Skills and Thinking Dispositions

Chris Unger
Heidi Goodrich
Harvard Graduate School of Education

A pilot investigation of the differences between students involved in the experimental Renaissance program (Renpro) and the Traditional program (Tradpro) was made in the fall of 1991, with a focus on the possibility of differences in domain understanding, group collaboration, and dispositions of thinking (Perkins, Jay & Tishman, 1991).

METHODOLOGY

A total of twelve groups of students were videotaped, nine groups consisting of three students and three groups consisting of two students. Half of these groups were assigned a science task, and half a history task. Half of these students the year before had attended the Renaissance program and half the Traditional program. Thirty-three students were tested altogether.

The history groups were given two contradictory accounts of an historical event—the "rescue" of Capt. John Smith by the Indian Pocahontas—and asked to interpret the event and the fact that there are two different accounts of it. The science groups were given a demonstration in which a can of Diet Coke and a can of regular Coke were placed in a pail of water. The Diet Coke floats at the surface of the water, while the regular Coke sinks to the bottom. The problem is figuring out and explaining why one floats and the other sinks. All students were asked to think about the problem for a few minutes, then share his or her ideas with the others. After these initial presentations, the students worked together toward a final take on the problem, which they presented to the researchers.

Each session was videotaped: The tapes were evaluated blind in terms of individual students' domain understanding, group collaboration, and thinking dispositions on a zero to three scale. The science instrument documents the quality of students' application of concepts of density in thinking about the floating/sinking phenomenon and evidence of their use of scientific inquiry. The history instrument documents the sophistication of students' interpretations of the fact that there are two differing accounts of the same event and the event itself, as well as the depth of their historical understanding.

The tapes were coded blind to student population, and four groups (two history and two science) were coded for reliability, which was moderately high. For history, reliability for historical understanding was 87%, for collaboration was 80%, and for thinking dispositions was 86%. For science, reliability for each variable was 83%.

RESULTS

History by Program

The Renpro students tended to receive higher scores on the Two Accounts (63% vs. 29% received a 2 and 0% vs. 13% received a 3) and Depth of Understanding variables (75% vs. 29% received a 2), but the Tradpro students tended to receive higher scores on the Event variable (86% vs. 38% received a 2). The Fisher's Exact Test show that no differences were significant at the p≤0.1 level.

More Tradpro students received a score of at least a 2 for group contribution, but more Renpro students received a 3 for group monitoring. Again, none of these differences were statistically significant.

The Renpro students tended to receive higher scores on three of the seven dispositions (Broad and Exploratory, Planful and Strategic, and Metacognitive) while the Tradpro students tended to receive higher scores on one (Intellectually Careful).

In sum, the Renpro students tended to receive higher scores on two of the three understanding variables and three of the seven disposition variables. The Tradpro students tended to receive higher scores for one of the understanding variables, both collaboration variables, and one of the thinking dispositions variables. None of these differences were statistically significant, however. All other differences between groups were mixed.

History by Honors

The Honors students tended to receive higher scores for both the Event (75% vs. 55% scored at least a 2) and the Depth (75% vs. 45% scored at least a 2) variables. In addition, slightly more Honors students received a 2 for the Two Accounts variable (50% vs. 45%). However, one non-Honors student (9%) received the highest score, a 3, for the Two Accounts variable.

Twenty-five percent of the Honors students received a score of 3 on the Group Contribution variable vs. 9% of non-Honors students who received an equally high score. For Group Monitoring, 75% of the Honors students scored at least a 2 vs. 45% of non-Honors students. Again, however, a lone student from the non-Honors group received a score of 3 for this variable.

On the Thinking Dispositions variables, the Honors population scored higher on all dispositions except for the disposition to be Planful and Strategic. Four of these differences were statistically significant: level 2 of Sustained Intellectual Curiosity (75% of the Honors students received at least a 2 versus 18% of non-Honors students); Clarify and Concretize (75% of the Honors students received at least a 2 versus 0% of non-Honors students): Intellectually Careful (50% of Honors students received at least a 2 versus 0% of the non-Honors students); and Metacognitive (50% of the Honors students receiving at least a 1 versus 0% of the non-Honors students).

Science by Program

The Renpro students again tended to receive higher scores than the Tradpro students for the science understanding variables. For the Density variable, 22% of the Renpro students received a score of 3 versus 0% of the Tradpro students, and 78%

of the Renpro students versus 55% of the Tradpro students scored at least a 2. Sixty-seven percent of the Renpro students versus 44% of the Tradpro students scored at least a level 2 on the Scientific Inquiry variable.

For the Group Monitoring variable, the Renpro students again performed slightly better. Fifty-six percent of the Renpro students versus 44% of the Tradpro students received a score of at least a 2, and 100% of the Renpro students versus 89% of the Tradpro students scored at least a 1.

On the Thinking Dispositions variables, the Renpro population tended to receive only slightly higher scores on five of the seven dispositions: Broad and Exploratory, Sustained Intellectual Curiosity, Planful and Strategic, Intellectually Careful, and Metacognitive.

In general, then, the Repro group did tend to perform better in each category of the science task; scientific understanding, group collaboration, and thinking dispositions.

Science by Honors

For the Density variable, 17% of the Honors students received a score of 3 versus 8% of the non-Honors students, and 83% of the Honors students versus 58% of the non-Honors students scored at least a 2. For the Scientific Inquiry variable, 33% of the Honors students and 0% of the non-Honors students received a 3, and 83% versus 42% scored at least a 2. The level 3 differences for Scientific Inquiry were found to be statistically significant.

For the Group Contribution variables, 50% of the Honors students received a score of 3 for the Group Contribution variable, versus 8% of non-Honors students. For the Group Monitoring variable, 33% of the Honors students scored a 3 versus 0% of non-Honors, and 67% of the Honors students scored at least a 2 versus 42% of the non-Honors students.

The Honors students received higher or at least equal scores on all seven dispositions. Eight of these differences were found to be significant: level 2 of Broad and Exploratory (67% versus 17%); level 3 of Sustained Intellectual Curiosity (33% versus 0%); levels 2 and 3 of Clarify and Concretize (67% versus 17% and 33% versus 0%); level 2 of Planful and Strategic (33% versus 0%); level 2 of Speculative and Playful (33% versus 0%); and levels 2 and 3 of Intellectually Careful (67% versus 8% and 33% versus 0%).

The Honors students then tended to receive higher scores in 25 or 33 levels on all 11 variables, including understanding, collaboration and dispositions. The between-group differences were statistically significant for certain levels of seven variables: 1) Scientific Inquiry, 2) the dispositions to be Broad and Exploratory, 3) Sustain Intellectual Curiosity, 4) Clarify and Concretize, 5) Planful and Strategic, 6) Speculative and Playful, and 7) Intellectually Careful.

SUMMARY

The differences between Renpro and Tradpro students are summarized on page 169. The Renpro students clearly performed better on more of these comparisons than did the Tradpro students, though none of these individual differences were statistically significant.

Differences by Program (Renpro vs. Tradpro)

History:

Renpro better

Interpretation of Two Accounts
Depth of Historical Understanding
Metacognitive
Broad and Exploratory
Speculative and Playful

Tradpro better

Interpretation of the Event
Group Contribution
Intellectually Careful

Science:

Renpro better

Understanding of Density
Understanding of Scientific Inquiry
Broad and Exploratory
Sustained Intellectual Curiosity
Planful and Strategic
Intellectually Careful
Metacognitive

Tradpro better

(none)

Overall:

Renpro better

Broad and Exploratory
Planful and Strategic
Speculative and Playful
Metacognitive

Tradpro better

Group Contribution

When the sign test was applied to these data collectively, the Renpro students performed significantly better than Tradpro students ($p<0.001$). When broken down by Honors, even greater differences were apparent. Not only did the Honors students receive higher or equal scores on every single level of every variable, but six of the differences in scores for thinking dispositions were statistically significant and the sign test indicated that Honors students were significantly higher ($p<0.001$) than the non-Honors students. It is worth noting that Honors students were drawn in equal numbers from the Renaissance and Traditional programs.

REFERENCES

Carroll, J. M. (1989). The Copernican Plan: Restructuring the American high school. Andover, MA: The Regional Laboratory for Educational Improvement of the Northeast and Islands.

Dweck, C.S. & Bempechat, J. (1983). Children's theories of intelligence: Consequences for learning. In S.G. Paris, G.M. Olson & H.W. Stevenson (Eds.). *Learning and motivation in the classroom.* Hillsdale, N.J.: Lawrence Erlbaum Associates.

Jagacinski, C.M. & Nicholls, J.G. (1987). Competence and affect in task involvement and ego involvement: The impact of social comparison information. *Journal of Educational Psychology,* 79, 107-114.

Nicholls, J.G. (1984). Achievement motivation: Conceptions of ability, subjective experience, task choice and performance. *Psychological Review*, 91, 328-346.

Perkins, D.N., Jay, E., & Tishman, S. (1991). Beyond abilities: A dispositional theory of thinking. Unpublished manuscript, Project Zero, Harvard Graduate School of Education, Cambridge, MA.

Weiner, B., Russell, D. & Lerman, D. (1972). The cognition-emotion process in achievement-related contexts. *Journal of Personality and Social Psychology*, 37, 1211-1220.